**An Intelligent Person's
Guide to Catholicism**

An Intelligent Person's Guide to Catholicism

Alban McCoy OFM Conv

continuum
LONDON • NEW YORK

Continuum

The Tower Building, 11 York Road, London SE1 7NX

15 East 26th Street, New York, NY 10010

British Library Cataloguing-in-Publication Data

A catalogue record for this book is available from the British Library.

ISBN 0 8264 7672 4

Hardback first published in 2001
Paperback first published in 2002
This edition published in 2005

All references to Conciliar documents are from *Decress of the Ecumenical Councils,* (ed. Norman Tanner SJ), Sheed & Ward and Georgetown University, 1990.

All references to the *Catechism of the Catholic Church* are from the Second Edition, Libreria Editrice Vaticana, 1997.

All references to the Code of Canon Law are from the New Revised English Translation, published in 1997 by HarperCollins

All scripture references are from the New Revised Standard Version.

Typeset by YHT, London
Printed and bound in Great Britain by Antony Rowe Ltd, Chippenham, Wiltshire

Contents

PART III THE SEVEN DEADLY SINS

PART IV THE VIRTUOUS LIFE

Introduction

Each of the brief chapters of this small book has its origin in a series of lunchtime talks given to all comers, but mainly undergraduates, at Fisher House, Cambridge, the home of the Catholic Chaplaincy to the University. They were delivered informally, as busy people hurriedly ate their lunch in between lectures and supervisions. But the distraction of food and haste did not deter the audience from close questioning and interested scrutiny of what was delivered. The value of those question sessions which followed the talks lay not least in the range of backgrounds from which the questioners came: medics, engineers, computer scientists, literature and language students, as well as philosophers and theologians were among those who regularly attended.

Of even more value and having direct relevance to the presentation of these talks under the present title was the persevering presence of many people from Christian denominations other than Catholic and of others belonging to no Christian persuasion. It was the presence of so many individuals genuinely interested to find out more about Catholicism that made the idea of publishing these talks initially plausible, despite my still not entirely dispelled doubts about their usefulness outside this original context. For confidence that these doubts might be misplaced I must thank my colleague at *The Tablet*, Lucy Lethbridge, who made the original suggestion that they should be published and Robin Baird-Smith at Continuum, whose experience and encouragement further diluted my reticence.

The original intention of these talks was to describe and explain in a straightforward and accessible way what Catholics believe and why. Of course, Christians of all denominations believe much in common, not least the central and defining doctrine of the Incarnation, that Jesus of Nazareth is God made man, the Word made flesh. But what distinguishes different Christian traditions is as much a matter of emphasis as doctrinal divergence. These talks sought to supply both the distinctive perspective and context within which Catholics characteristically understand the beliefs they share with other Christians and those doctrines peculiar to Catholics. In the form in which they are presented here they are intended to fulfil the same function: that is, to render intelligible those aspects of Catholicism one might reasonably assume to be foundational.

Medieval authors customarily spoke of the *preambula fidei*, preliminaries of faith. Fully recognizing that faith is a gift of God, not the work of human invention or ingenuity or persuasion, these authors nevertheless sought to clear away obstacles to faith by showing that what is proposed for belief was not unreasonable or incoherent. This essay fits into that category and is intended to afford initial access to the most basic aspects of Catholic faith and practice.

It goes without saying that this brief essay lays claim neither to comprehensiveness nor originality: it is neither a catechism nor a theological tract. The topics covered reflect the kinds of questions which it seems to me intelligent and informed enquirers, as well as Catholics themselves, most frequently ask about Catholicism at the present time. I have sought, in other words, to be topical.

Nobody knowledgeable about Catholicism from within will find anything new here. Indeed, much will be familiar. It is in that sense derivative, drawing upon many sources, with only occasional reference to the many authors to whom one owes the formation of one's own ideas and understanding.

An older style of apologetics sought to demonstrate the truth of Christian claims. Such an enterprise is now, not unreasonably, deemed not only unfashionable but counter-productive in an undeniably pluralistic world. The hallmark of our present situation is not so much a crisis of belief as a crisis of intelligibility. Many who reject Christian faith in general and Catholicism in particular reject not what has seemed to them unbelievable but what has come across as simply unintelligible. If the claims of Catholic Christianity are to get a fair hearing they must first be given a fair rendering in terms intelligible to the world.

For my mother
and my late father

PART I

Common Questions

FAITH AND REASON : ENEMIES OR ALLIES?

> 'I can't believe that', said Alice. 'Can't you?' the Queen said in a
> pitying tone. 'Try again: draw a long breath and shut your eyes.'
> Alice laughed. 'There's no use trying,' she said. 'One can't
> believe impossible things.' 'I dare say you haven't had much
> practice', said the Queen. 'Why, sometimes I've believed as
> many as six impossible things before breakfast.'

When Lewis Carroll wrote this tart piece of dialogue between
Alice and the imperious Red Queen, he had in mind much-pub-
licized satirical jibes about the doctrine of infallibility only
recently promulgated at the First Vatican Council in 1870. But
'believing in impossible things' is exactly how many would now
characterize the position not just of Catholics but of religious
believers in general. Where such a conviction is rooted in reflective consideration rather than unthinking prejudice, this view of
religious belief is often associated with an assumption shared,
consciously or unconsciously, by many of our contemporaries;
namely, that reason deals with objective and publicly verifiable
facts, while faith is concerned with subjective and privately
owned states of mind. Reason, in other words, points us in the
direction of knowledge, while faith leads us in the direction of,
at best, emotion and, at worst, superstition.

That would be the view, albeit baldly stated, of many who
count themselves unbelievers. But the underlying assumption –
that faith and reason are opposed and contrary activities, pointing
in opposite directions and leading to incompatible conclusions
– is not confined to unbelievers. It is shared by many who would
certainly count themselves believers and, more specifically,
Christian believers. They too would hold that faith and reason

are opposed and have no relevance to one another. But they would express this disjunction differently: their view would be that belief has no need of reason. Indeed, reason is positively dangerous and must at all costs be subordinated to faith and belief.

For all their differences, what these strange and unlikely bedfellows have in common is their disavowal of any continuity or community between faith and reason. The view that reason, as opposed to faith, is pre-eminent in all matters that engage human interest and understanding is usually associated with groups openly hostile to religious belief such as the British Rationalist Society of Great Britain and prominent individuals engaged in promoting the exclusive claims of science who, with almost religious zeal, miss no opportunity to dismiss what they take to be the counter-claims of religion. Many of these would see themselves in direct descent from the empiricism of the Scottish philosopher David Hume (1711–76), (though his strictures were as undermining of scientific method as of religious belief and practice) and the positivism of the now defunct Logical Positivists. 'Reason alone' was the leitmotif of the Enlightenment as the *philosophes* in the eighteenth century sought to free men and women from the slavery of superstition and, more recently, the youthful A. J. Ayer's repeatedly reprinted *Language, Truth and Logic* proclaimed that religious assertions were neither true nor false, just meaningless.

Those, on the other hand, who would hold the contrary view, namely that faith, not reason, is pre-eminent in all matters of ultimate importance, represent a strand within Christianity that appeared early on in the history of the Church and has waxed and waned ever since. Even St Paul himself was, on occasion, ambiguous about the relations which should obtain between philosophy and Christianity.[1]

But in the early Church the most vociferous and eloquent voice raised against any association between reason and faith was that of the great African theologian Tertullian (c.AD 160–220). He openly questioned the believer's need of philosophy or any other knowledge. He was convinced that the believer, albeit by the grace of God, has all the answers: or, at least, the answers that matter. 'After Christ Jesus, we have no need of curiosity; after the Gospel we need no inquiry.'[2]

'Faith alone' (*sola fides*) was the battle-cry of the Protestant

Reformation in the sixteenth century, and in the century just past the great Swiss Protestant theologian Karl Barth, thundered his critique of his co-religionists who had wandered from this pure Reformation doctrine.

Now such anti-intellectualism is inconsistent with historic, authentic, Catholic Christianity. The Catholic tradition has never seen any inherent conflict between faith and reason. And this is part of the wider Catholic insight that nature, everything that exists (as opposed to the use of the word by ecologists to designate a certain part of what exists, namely, the natural world) is, by definition, created by God and for God and is, therefore, good, even if damaged by sin. This applies as much to human activities and faculties as to everything else; so St Thomas Aquinas can say that grace does not destroy or replace nature but builds on it and perfects it.

Now the alleged antithesis between faith and reason, on which both the anti-intellectualism of the fideist and the scientism of the secular humanist depend, is premised on a misunderstanding of *both* faith *and* reason. I would argue that there is no reason without faith, and no faith without reason: they are inextricably connected. They appear disjoined and opposed only when reason is understood in the narrow sense of positivism and faith is understood in the narrow sense of fideism. In other words, both reason and faith, in these views, have been distorted into equally stultifying and equally barren fundamentalisms. Notice, in passing (and we'll come back to this) how both positions – the rationalist and the fideist – trade on the tendency to feel happier with views that are of the 'either-or' variety, as opposed to the 'both-and' kind. In reality, both faith and reason are much richer concepts and activities than these two atavistic positions allow.

The view that religious belief is and must remain an entirely separate and distinct activity from any rational and intellectual endeavour, is the single most damaging distortion that infects and undermines the confidence of Christians to engage boldly with human perplexity through orderly thinking and intelligent enquiry. It leads inexorably to the conviction that religious faith, being immune to reason and argument, has no place in public debate and discussion where we strive honestly and truthfully to exercise our critical faculties. On this view of faith, religious belief cannot but appear among those things to be grown out of as soon as possible. Rather like the Red Queen's position in *Through the Looking Glass*, belief requires, if not a lobotomy, then at least a suspension of our powers of reasoning.

Now this fideist position which is, as I said, inconsistent with historic, authentic, Catholic Christianity, was definitively repudiated by the incomparable St Augustine of Hippo in late antiquity. Much later, in the thirteenth century, St Thomas Aquinas was the first theologian and philosopher to show the complete harmony of faith and reason, while keeping them formally and materially distinct. And the much-misunderstood Decree of the First Vatican Council in 1870 stating that it was possible to know of God's existence through reason apart from faith was a reassertion of the belief that reason and faith have one origin and one goal: namely, God.

Now more often than not, in the history of Christianity, people have lapsed into fideism in an attempt to defend Christian belief from its enemies. They have retreated behind the barricades by insulating belief from reason and argument. But, in practice, this has never worked: it may lead to tolerance of religious belief, but at the cost of being regarded as nothing more than a mildly interesting eccentricity. But, even more disastrously, it removes Christian belief from where it belongs and where it located itself from the very beginning: namely, the public domain of rational and reasonable argument and debate, engaging with the questions and aspirations of real people in real life.

The Christian intellectual tradition developed precisely because believers wanted both to understand their faith with the mind as well as the heart and to communicate and share it with other rational beings. Both of these goals were plausible because Christians were convinced that the faith they had received was both a *reasonable* conviction: that is, it was able to stand its own ground in the context of rational and humane argument; and that it was a conviction that was *communicable,* in the language and thought-forms of their own time.

So it was precisely their own desire to understand and their willingness to enter into sustained and serious dialogue with unbelievers on their own terms that initiated the tradition of rational theology which we now take for granted. The only alternative to finding ways of expressing the faith in terms that were intelligible to their own contemporaries was to fall into parochialism and intellectual obscurantism. And since this message of hope they had received was meant for everyone – hence, the *Catholic* Church – this latter path was not an option.

As a matter of simple historical fact, once it had moved beyond the original Jewish communities in which it came to birth, the Church developed a theology and a self-understanding that was profoundly influenced by and made possible through its use of prevailing Greek philosophy and, in particular, though not exclusively, Platonism.[3] The use made of such concepts and ideas by early Christian thinkers was unavoidable if it was to proclaim the Christian Gospel in ways intelligible to a Greek world – which was, of course, also their own world.

But it must also be said influences were not in one direction only: Greek philosophy was influenced by Christian insights. Indeed, Western civilization, as such, could be said to result from the confluence of, on the one hand, the speculative power of Greek philosophy and, on the other hand, the new and original religious values and insights of Christianity.[4]

But this cultural accommodation was not just a temporary strategy: it is a permanent necessity. Every age must find the best ways of faithfully conveying the truths of Christian faith, using whatever is available and appropriate from the surrounding culture. Inevitably, the philosophies of a given age, in which contemporary aspirations and questions are expressed and through which we all understand ourselves, will be one of the chief resorts to which theology turns for ways of understanding and expressing the Christian hope.

This is one reason – and a very important one – why we need to be aware of the philosophical roots of many of the concepts theology uses. Without this understanding, we will not be able to distinguish between the form and content of any theological statement. And if we are unable to do that, there is a real danger that we will become trapped in one particular, historically conditioned expression of faith which, with the passage of time, may lose its effective meaning, answering questions nobody is asking and widening the gap between its message and its medium. The Dominican theologian Fergus Kerr expresses the problem aptly:

> There can be no constructive theology – because there can be no constructive thought on any matter of human concern – without a measure of philosophical reflection. Certainly if theologians work in the belief that they are doing without philosophy, they will simply be the prisoners of whatever philosophy was dominant thirty years earlier – or 350 years earlier.[5]

This delusion has far-reaching consequences for Christianity, not least in making it impossible to convey and recommend Christian faith to the contemporary world as an intelligible and intelligent enterprise.

GOD AND PROOF: ARGUMENT OR ASSERTION?

We moderns place great weight on 'proof'. This is because an ideal of mathematical certainty, which for the Greeks belonged quite properly within the context of logic, has since the sixteenth century and at no time more that in our own era – at least until recently – come to be thought of as the paradigm of true knowledge to which we are taught to aspire and against which we are taught to judge everything.

But this extrapolation of a perfectly legitimate and intelligible objective from one context into all contexts has serious consequences for our understanding of other areas of our lives. In practice, this notion of proof and certainty is quite different from the way the words function in much else that is important to us, especially in the area of personal knowledge and the conduct of our relationships with other people on all kinds of levels.

Consider, for example, how we understand 'proof' in ordinary, everyday life. In general, outside the mathematics lecture or the laboratory, we only prove those things we already believe to be true. We prove that we have paid our fare on the bus by showing our ticket; we prove to ourselves and others that we can do something; we prove our innocence of a crime; we prove that we are not mad. All these are retrospective proofs.

The same must be said about alleged 'proofs' for God's existence. But they are significantly different from proofs in general because to prove the existence of God is to prove, first and foremost, a negative, not a positive. That is to say, to prove that God exists is to prove that some questions must remain permanently unanswered. It is to prove that there is a question that will always impose itself upon us, no matter how far our knowledge of the world advances, because it is a question that the very existence of the world raises: a question arising not from the way the world is but from the fact that there is a world at all, as opposed to there being nothing.

There is a parallel here with the way one might seek to prove that some particular discipline or, indeed, science in general, is a valid and intelligible intellectual activity. Here one would seek to demonstrate that there are questions to be asked under this heading, understanding to be gained by pursuing this discipline. By extension, one is proving the point of questioning, as such.

To 'prove' the existence of God is, therefore, quite different both from merely asserting one's belief that God exists and from arriving at conclusions inferred from premises. I may say 'I believe that God exists' without need of proof. It is either true or false that this is my belief. But to speak of proving God's existence is to discuss, not whether I believe, but what grounds I have for such belief. It is, in other words, to render my belief intelligible, both to myself and to others.

How do I do this? By showing that the word 'God' makes sense, has a legitimate and intelligible use and place in intelligent and intelligible discourse. And I show this by showing the legitimacy of a question beneath all other questions, a question raised by questioning itself, a question posed by the world and the existence of everything. The word 'God' is used to refer to whatever it is that answers this question.

What is this question? It can be formulated in various ways, but this is perhaps the most succinct: 'How come anything rather than nothing?' Some have doubted the validity of this question. But is it not anomalous to consider it quite valid and legitimate to ask 'How come?' of any particular thing or event in the world and yet to outlaw or regard as invalid the same question concerning everything – all existence?

The question is: is there an unanswered question about the existence of the world – not about how the world is in this or that particular regard – but that it is? Can we be puzzled by the existence of the world instead of nothing? I can be and I am: and this is to be puzzled about God. To prove the existence of God, therefore, is first and foremost to demonstrate, to render intelligible and intelligent, precisely this puzzlement.

Are such arguments and proofs alternatives to faith? No. Rational argument does not create belief. But it most certainly creates a climate without which belief cannot flourish.[6] Speaking of the proofs, the late Bernard Lonergan said that 'Though they may not make people believe, they may still convince the converted that they are not crazy.'[7]

We can summarize the role of so-called proofs for God's existence, understood as arguments in justification of theological discourse:

- They demonstrate the insufficiency of the universe to account for its own existence.
- They demonstrate the validity of a question underlying all other questions.
- They demonstrate the intelligibility of talk of 'God'.
- They display the logical space occupied by the word 'God' understood as 'the beginning and end of all things'.
- They begin from our (varied and changing) ways of understanding the world (cosmological) or from understanding *tout court* (ontological).
- They predispose for faith – rather than create it – by clearing away obstacles and thus creating a climate for faith.
- They begin from the fundamental assumptions of a given horizon.
- They articulate transcendence.
- Alone, they never convince others who do not believe.
- They do not afford independent or alternative access to God but they do help us to realize we are not crazy to believe.

When most people think of proofs for God's existence, the so-called Five Ways of St Thomas Aquinas come to mind. But of all the writings of Aquinas these are perhaps the most misunderstood. This is doubtless due to the fact that they are more often than not wrenched from their context in a seamless theological treatise and included in excerpts from the whole corpus or as readings in collections of texts in the field of philosophy of religion.

A more accurate understanding of the Five Ways is an example of what I have described above: a rational demonstration of the way the word 'God' is to be used, namely, whatever it is that accounts for the existence of everything, that which is the beginning and end of everything.

But it must be stressed that the word 'God' is not offered as an answer in any straightforward sense to the question raised by the existence of everything. It conveys no information except as a point of departure for inference; nor must it be understood as an explanation of the world and how it is in this or that particular regard. In the Five Ways, Aquinas does indeed demonstrate that there is an explanation but he also demonstrates why it is that we have no access to it by our own unaided reason. It is part of the very meaning and use of the word 'God' that it refers to what transcends everything: including our understanding.

The Five Ways, then, do nothing to remove the puzzlement or dispel the mystery of why there is anything rather than nothing. On the contrary, they draw our attention to this mystery by showing it to be unavoidable. They thus show that the word 'God' has both an intelligible reference and an essential place in reflective human discourse. The upshot is to demonstrate that Christian theology is a reasonable and acceptable intellectual pursuit.

It might be useful to conclude this chapter with a short statement of the structure of the Five Ways in Aquinas's *Summa Theologiae* 1a. 2.

1. There is some pervasive feature about things as we find them that gives rise to a question. Each of the Five Ways takes for its starting-point one such feature, namely, things are (i) changing (ii) dependent (iii) perishable (iv) limited (v) directed.

2. Explanations of these features (answers to the question) in terms of the existence of things within our intellectual framework, while perfectly adequate at their own level, imply further explanation (raise further questions) at another level.

3. Such further explanation can only be expressed negatively since it is in terms of the existence of what is outside the scope of our understanding (cannot be expressed by the meanings of our words). At this level, the answer is in terms of the existence of what is <u>un</u>changing, <u>in</u>dependent, <u>non</u>-perishable, <u>un</u>limited, and <u>not</u> directed by another.

4. This is what people mean by 'God'.

'GOD' AND GOD: LANGUAGE OR REALITY?

Aristotle comments in his *De Coelo* that small errors at the beginning of our thinking lead to vast errors in our conclusions. Nowhere is this more the case than in our grasp of the correct and incorrect uses of the word 'God'. Errors here lead inexorably to fundamental and far-reaching distortions (practical as well as intellectual) in our understanding of everything concerning the propositions of faith including how we understand ourselves. And it's this misunderstanding more than any other that has generated the false dichotomies and pseudo-questions that seem to cast doubt on the intelligibility of religious belief and Christianity in particular.

More specifically, the most dangerous potential distortion in our understanding of the word 'God' is anthropomorphism. This danger has been recognized throughout the history of Christianity. Indeed, sensitivity to this conceptual confusion antedates Christianity: it was noted as early as the sixth century BC when Xenophanes, the pre-Socratic philosopher, mocked the all-too-human ideas of the gods cherished by different races according to their own characteristics. He even commented that if donkeys had gods doubtless they would be thought to have long ears and snouts.

Learning from both Greek philosophy and the Old Testament, Christians quickly came to see in anthropomorphism the intellectual equivalent of the sin of idolatry. And later, in the context of medieval theology and philosophy, it was universally acknowledged that in talk of God we find ourselves perched between, on the one hand, anthropomorphism, which ultimately reduces the divine to the status of a magnified human worldly reality, and an agnosticism which reminds us that when we talk about God we can never know fully what we mean by the words we use, nor do we know how the concepts we apply to him, borrowed as they are from the familiar world of our experience, make true reference to him. But of these two extremes it was always recognized that agnosticism was less perilous than anthropomorphism.

It was the prevalence of this tendency of the human mind towards anthropomorphism that fuelled the views of Ludwig Feuerbach in the nineteenth century. In his *The Essence of*

Christianity, which was avidly read by Karl Marx, he suggested that 'God' was a projection of the human mind in its need of security and consolation.

But it is central to the Catholic Christian tradition that God the Creator transcends his creation. 'There is no one who can give a name to the ineffable God and if anyone dares to say there is one, he suffers from an incurable madness.' (Justin Martyr, *First Apology* 61). And the Fourth Lateran Council in 1215 decreed that 'God is eternal, infinite, and unchangeable, incomprehensible, almighty and ineffable . . .' (*cap1: On the Catholic Faith,* in Tanner, vol. 1, p. 230)

The starting-point for understanding why it must be so that God is an ineffable mystery, permanently beyond the reach of both our language and our understanding and exceeding whatever we can know about him, is to remember that the most basic use of the word, its foundational sense, is to designate the Creator of all that exists: the source of existence itself. Failure to grasp this and all it entails leads inexorably to anthropomorphism. The Creator of everything must, of necessity, transcend everything. Thus the apophatic tradition (from the Greek, *apophemi* – I deny; hence, the 'way of denial' or, in medieval terminology, the *via negativa*) within Christianity sought to articulate and preserve this transcendence. Indeed, some would say that this is the crucial role of doctrine as such: Nicholas Lash, former Norris-Hulse Professor of Divinity at Cambridge, speaks of 'protocols against idolatry'.[8] And his predecessor, Donald Mackinnon, has it that:

Perhaps it is the central task of theology in this age and generation to face anew the question of what sort of silence, what sort of repudiation of every sort of image best conveys the ultimacy not of judgment but of love.[9]

A clear understanding of what it means to speak of God as Creator will help us to avoid anthropomorphism. But it will also help us to see that there can be no conflict or contradiction between any scientific research concerning processes which give rise to the universe as we know it and the notion of God in classical theism as articulated by Aquinas and others.

Despite its centrality to the Christian theistic tradition, however, many believers as well as unbelievers have failed and continue to fail to take the transcendence of God seriously. Some would associate this emphasis with an intellectually 'soft' attachment to mystification, complaining that it opens the door to intolerable vagueness. Others find it difficult to accept on other grounds. It is commonly assumed, for instance, that theology is premised on knowledge and understanding of the nature and attributes of God, just as we might have knowledge and understanding of some individual person within the world. Indeed, many speak uncontroversially of God in the context of philosophy of religion as a 'person', where what is meant is something like a person in a human context, namely a centre of consciousness, with beliefs and thoughts, just like ours in essence but of a superior kind. A third source of unease with this insistence on God's transcendence arises from the alleged corollary to this view that God is a distant, unfeeling deity, unaffected by the things of this world, including its suffering, and therefore inconsistent with the God of the Bible and especially of the New Testament.

But any wavering over this notion of God's transcendence, for whatever reason, constitutes a radical departure from traditional Christian talk of God as in the thought of such giants of Christian thinking as Augustine, Anselm, Bonaventure and Aquinas and Luther. Such a domestication of the notion of God enters into Christian discourse in the late seventeenth century, in the wake of the burgeoning new sciences and the growing confidence in the human capacity to understand everything under the rubric of science, including God. For classical Christian theism God is ineffable, incomparable and incomprehensible. And this is not merely the assertion that it is difficult to understand God. God defies human understanding in principle, not just in practice, because he transcends our mode of thought entirely: he belongs to no class, nor is he an individual item of the universe.

But it may now be objected that in the Christian view, the Incarnation, being the revelation of God, surely eases the mystery and renders God intelligible by giving us knowledge of the divine essence or nature. St Thomas, for one, would reject such ideas. That which is apprehended in faith is as much a mystery as that which results from the searchings of unaided reason. The object of divine faith, in other words, is still the Unseen and Unknown.[10] God is thus no less unknown to the believer and, in a sense, to the Christian believer he is more, rather than less, mysterious. Mackinnon wrote that it was precisely the Incarnation which effectively renders nonsensical any anthropomorphic understanding of God. 'It is Jesus of Nazareth who manifests the divine transcendence as present in Himself, in those places in which his humanity might be thought at first sight most completely to obscure it.'[11] And Hans Urs von Balthasar makes a similar point, at greater length.

> . . . it is precisely in this light [of the Incarnation] that for the first time and definitively we grasp the true incomprehensibility of God. It is here that God breaks for ever all the 'wisdom' of the world by the 'folly' of his love which chooses men without reason, by his entering into the chaos of the history of humanity, by his bearing the guilt of his lost and fallen creatures. This incomprehensible love of the God who acts in the event of Christ raises him far above all the incomprehensibility of philosophical notions of God which consist simply in the fact of negating all statements about God, which may be ventured on the grounds of our knowledge of the world, out of regard for historical otherness. But this more powerful incomprehensibility of the biblical God only remains in effect, so long as the dogmatic formulae protect it against renewed attempts at rationalisation. The folly of the love of God – this is where we meet true mystery. And here is communion, not knowledge, agape not gnosis.[12]

The Good News of salvation made known in the person of Christ, the revelation of God, serves not to increase our knowledge of God's nature but to enable us to enter into communion with him. Of course, we are enabled also to say things and to know things we otherwise would not know through reason. We know that God is a communion of persons and, most crucially, we know that he loves what he has created and has created it out of love. But to know that *anybody* loves you, let alone the Creator of all things, can hardly be thought of as ordinary knowledge and much less mere information. The role of all our talk of God in the form of doctrine is, therefore, to help us 'set our hearts on God (and not on some thing which we mistake for God) and to make true mention of Him'. [13]

GOD: THREE AND ONE?

God is infinite, we are finite. He is a mystery, unfathomable and always beyond the reach of our minds. This does not mean that we cannot know anything at all about God, but that we cannot know what it takes to be God, we cannot know his nature or essence.

When we turn to the Trinity all we have said about the mystery of God deepens. Our words become even more inadequate. But in the doctrine of the Trinity we come to see that the distance between God and man is bridged not by knowledge but by love, his for us, and our sharing in the love of Father, Son and Holy Spirit.

The Trinity is the central mystery of the Christian faith from which derive all the other mysteries and doctrines. And this mystery is known to us only because it is revealed to us: it is not the result of human inventiveness and is not a construction of the human mind.

The doctrine of the Trinity did not, however, drop from the sky nor was it culled ready-made from the Old Testament. But nor is it a completed theory about God that answers all questions, much less an explanation of how the Divinity works or an insight into the domestic arrangements of the Deity. It emerged in response to doctrinal challenges about the divine status of Jesus. It was hammered out in the course of a life and death struggle to think out this revelation, this self-disclosure of God, as a coherent whole.

Technical terms were employed to state as clearly as possible both what cannot be true of God and what must be asserted of him. These terms are necessarily inadequate and they certainly don't claim to explain how it can be so that God is both three and one. (No more does the term 'transubstantiation' explain how bread and wine become the body and blood of our Lord: it rather makes clearer what is being asserted in this doctrine against counter-claims and misrepresentations.) In this sense, the doctrine of the Trinity as formulated by the Church is a collection of technical decisions which guard Christian thinking from errors of various kinds and suggest fruitful lines of thought and speech and practice for those who believe.

The starting-point for the doctrine is the conviction that Jesus of Nazareth is God. This is the central conviction that gives rise to the Church as the community of faith gathered round its Lord. But this belief had to be related to the firmly held monotheism of the Judaism that forms the background to Christian faith.

A further stage in this development comes when, reflecting on what Jesus himself had taught and promised and upon their own experience of faith and communion with one another and with the Father and the Son, Christians came to the conviction that their understanding of the Godhead would be incomplete without recognizing that what makes this life of faith possible is the presence among them of the Spirit promised by our Lord. This, they came to believe, is the imparting by the Father and the Son of their own love. So it is that though we, who are inevitably remote from the public events by however many years of time and in however many other ways, are nevertheless exposed to what was done then and to the One who did it. 'No one', says St Paul, 'can say: "Jesus is Lord", except by the Holy Spirit.'

So the Trinity begins with the conviction that Jesus is God, and is grounded in the complex human experience of redemption. But what exactly is the doctrine of the Trinity and what does it entail for us now in our own lives? The teaching, put simply, is that there is only one God and that this God reveals himself and is known to us as Father, Son and Holy Spirit: three persons, distinct and yet each entirely God. They are distinct in all that pertains to them as persons, but united perfectly as a single Deity. God is a unity of substance, a diversity of persons.

These three persons, however, are not three ingredients or three elements making up, by addition, a single reality. This is not, in other words, merely an intriguing mathematical conundrum. One way of thinking about the doctrine of the Trinity is as an explication of the assertion that God is love. It spells out what it would mean to say that love is the deepest and most basic reality of all.

Jesus is God. God is love. God is, therefore, in some sense demanded by the nature of love, a relationship. The Trinity is love given, love received, and loved shared. And the Christian life is a sharing, made possible by sanctifying grace, in this divine love.

St Augustine, the greatest writer on these questions in the West, uses various images and illustrations to explain the doctrine. He uses first and foremost our experience of love and he uses the image of the human mind which knows itself and loves itself. The basic strategy of Augustine is to uncover the image of the Trinity in our own lives. After all, if we are made in the image and likeness of God we are made in the image and likeness of the Trinity.

And so in the experience of human love there is complete oneness and yet the distinctness that comes from being loved. Love unites precisely by affirming and upholding the dignity of the person as an individual. We don't smother the people we love; we actually affirm their separate existence from us. Without this respect there simply cannot be communion, because communion implies the union of two distinct and discrete individuals.

So the doctrine of the Trinity is foundational not only for our understanding of God but also for our understanding of ourselves and our lives. But notice: what is communicated to us in this revelation is not neutral information, residing only in the intellect, no more than the knowledge that comes from love is mere information. This is God's own self-disclosure and it has only one purpose: to invite us to share in his life, the divine love which is the Blessed Trinity.

GOD AND EVIL: CAN THEY BOTH EXIST?

Of all the ambiguities and contradictions with which we live, the fact of evil in a world allegedly created by not just a good God but a loving God, is surely the most perplexing. This is far more than a theological and philosophical problem, a merely intellectual puzzle. As Dostoevsky reminds us in *The Brothers Karamazov*, it is 'a problem which must touch the soul of every sensitive religious person'. For many it is also one of the most serious obstacles to Christian faith. But is the fact of evil in the world inconsistent with the existence of a good and omnipotent God? And what light is shed on our understanding of evil by Christianity's startling conviction that the God who has created and who, from moment to moment, sustains this world in existence, has revealed himself and his love precisely in the worst excess of human evil? The Cross is at once the greatest evil and the greatest good and it is here that we are given grounds for believing that the mystery of sin and evil is within the providence of God, however little we may understand how this might be so. In other words, without understanding how, we are enabled to know that this mystery is resolved in the even greater mystery of God's providential love. But first we need to draw some distinctions.

As commonly discussed, the so-called 'problem of evil' takes two quite different forms, one theoretical, the other practical. The first of these forms is a philosophical problem formulated as an intellectual dilemma. Traditionally, it claims that, given the fact of evil, it necessarily follows that either God does not exist or, if he does, then far from being good, he is an uncaring and callous monster, who has created an equally callous and pitilessly uncaring world.

This traditional form of the philosophical problem has changed little since it was first formulated by Epicurus (370– 341 BC) in the fourth century before Christ. The same argument was given deadly precision in the eighteenth century by the Scottish empiricist David Hume who concluded: 'Epicurus's old questions are still unanswered. Is he willing to prevent evil, but unable? Then he is impotent. Is he able, but not willing? Then he is malevolent. Is he both able and willing? Whence then is evil?'[14] The same reasoning continues in our own day to hold many back from belief.

What is being claimed in all forms of the philosophical problem of evil is that evil makes a nonsense of the idea of a good and all-powerful God: it is, in other words, a direct challenge to the intelligibility of faith in God.

No matter how we view the first form of the problem of evil none of us can escape the second form of the problem: that is the experience of evil. The practical or pastoral problem of evil is, in this sense, an unavoidable part of the very fabric of human experience. How are we to cope in a world where evil seems inevitable? Apart from the actual pain of evil, whether physical or mental, the sheer fact of human suffering, whether caused by nature or human wickedness, whether our own or the observed experiences of others, can at times fill us with a fear that makes life unbearable. Doubts about God's existence frequently accompany tragedy when it touches us personally.

This second form of the problem of evil, then, is a problem of meaning and purpose. Only the conviction that evil can never be the final word, that no evil can lead to the ultimate compromise of anything that is for the good, can ease the sense of futility that so easily arises in the face of evil. Without this, life would surely be, as Macbeth says, no more than 'a tale told by an idiot, full of sound and fury, signifying nothing' (*Macbeth* V. v. 16). Even if we cannot make sense of the experience of evil, we need some ground for hope. Without hope, we cannot live.

It will be obvious that, in order to address this second form of the problem of evil, our attention will be directed not only to arguments but to events at the heart of faith: only in appreciating the significance of these events can the mystery of evil be seen in an appropriate perspective. But what we shall find is not a solution in any straightforward sense, nor an argument to dispel difficulty, but grounds for hope and confidence. The mystery, however, must remain intact. Christianity does not offer us an opiate or anaesthetic to take away the painful perplexity of human existence. On the contrary, it will expose us to the very heart of this mystery and to its most explicit realization in the Cross of Christ, at one and the same time both the greatest evil and the greatest good.

But now we need to make a further distinction. Evil can be divided into two kinds. There is the evil which we usually call natural evil or evil suffered. This is the kind we refer to when we think of the tragedy and devastation that come upon us in the form of wind, fire, flood and human error. Then there is the evil which we usually refer to as moral evil or evil done. Here we are thinking of our own loosing of evil on the world through human choices and actions. This is the evil *we* do, the religious short-hand for which is 'sin'.

Turning, then, to the first form of the problem: does the existence of evil disprove or, at least, count heavily against the existence of a good God? The contradiction between the existence of evil and the existence of God gains plausibility from two confusions: confusion about what precisely is being referred to when we speak of evil and confusion about ways in which we can and ways in which we cannot use the word 'God'. These confusions are not confined to those who find the problem of evil an obstacle to faith. They are common among many who profess belief in God and especially by many who confidently construct elab-

orate and elegant theodicies (justifications of God as a solution
to the problem of evil) in an attempt to defend God against his
detractors. I shall argue that, given an intelligible account of the
meaning of the word 'God', no such theodicy can be constructed
and none, indeed, is needed even if it could. It is significant that
theodicies of this kind, that is, attempts to solve the problem of
evil, begin only in the seventeenth century, at the same time, as
I have said, that unease is felt about the insistence that God is
beyond our knowledge and understanding.

What do we mean by 'evil'? To what do we refer when we
speak of evil? Whenever and in whatever context we speak of
evil, without exception, we are referring to a defect or a deficiency. Now, rather than a thing in itself, a defect or a deficiency is an aspect of something else. There are defective things,
deeds, situations. In all these cases, we mean there is something
missing. This will be more obvious to us if we consider what we
commonly, though not entirely accurately, take to be the opposite of evil, namely, good.

Whenever we use the words 'good' or 'goodness', we are
speaking analogically: that is to say that, though there is a common meaning for the word stretching across all its uses, it nevertheless also means different things in different contexts. And
what exactly it means in each context will depend on what thing
is being described as good and what our expectations of that
thing are. We know what we expect of a good dishwasher or a
good pair of shoes or a good dinner and our expectations are
both similar and different in each case. What makes a good dishwasher good is that it hygienically and efficiently washes dish-
es, runs quietly, and disposes of the water efficiently, etc. A
wholly different set of qualities would be expected of a good pair
of shoes or a good dinner. But unless I know *what* something is,
I won't know what to expect of it and, therefore, I will not know
whether it's good or bad. To say of something that it is bad is to
say that it does not come up to our expectations: it is not what it
should be. It is, in other words, deficient in some way or other.
Badness, therefore, is fundamentally a lack of something which
should be there, given the nature of the particular thing in question. This is what both St Augustine and St Thomas Aquinas
mean when they say that evil is a *privatio boni*: a certain absence
of good.

But it is important to see what they are *not* saying here. They are not saying that badness consists in just any absence or lack whatever. It is an absence of what belongs to the nature of that which is being described as bad. So, for instance, we would not judge as bad a dishwasher that could not iron clothes. So evil consists, strictly speaking, in the absence of a quality or characteristic, a good, in other words, which should be present in a thing because it is the kind of thing that it is.

Again, to say this is *not* to say, as do Christian Scientists, for example, after their founder, Mary Baker Eddy, that evil is an illusion, something entirely unreal. Evil certainly is *not* something in itself – it is a gap in something else – but it is certainly *not* an illusion. For instance, to take a famous example, a hole in your sock does not consist in anything at all – it is the absence of wool or cotton or whatever. But holes in socks are thoroughly real.[15] What matters, however, is *where* the absence, in this case a hole, is.

An important implication of this view is that since what we call evil or badness is a lack in something that exists and since the fundamental meaning of 'good' and 'goodness' must be what exists fully and thus fulfils its nature, there can be nothing that is entirely bad or evil. This would be a contradiction: something that was entirely bad would not exist at all. But the converse is not a contradiction. That is, some things can be entirely good: that is, entirely what they should be, existing fully according to their nature. Evil, then, is always rooted in some good and existing thing.

Having tried to be clear about what we mean, strictly speaking, by evil and badness, we can now turn to see how this applies to the occurrence of natural evil in the world, that is, evil suffered. Remember that here we mean the features of the physical environment which, most often in times of disaster, we want to call evil. First, natural evil is always associated with some good. What we call evil is a consequence or concomitant of what is good, seen from another point of view. So, for instance, to use a famous example from Aquinas, when the lion devours the lamb, this is very bad news for the lamb but extremely good news for the lion. It actually means that the lion can go on being a good, healthy lion fulfilling its nature and ensuring the continuance of its species. We all agree this is a good thing.

Or when a volcano erupts, this can be very bad for anybody who is in the wrong place at the wrong time. And yet such a phenomenon is very necessary for the rest of the earth's surface and the stability of the whole planet in general. Interestingly, if the eruption takes place on a distant island where it can be viewed in safety, far from speaking of evil, we marvel at the splendour of the natural world.

Now this inevitable entailment of consequences and concomitants applies throughout the natural world, which includes ourselves, of course. If you want some good things, like lions, you have to accept some 'bad' things, 'bad' from a particular point of view, that is, like lambs, or whatever, being eaten. This complementarity and correspondence is a characteristic of a material universe which exists in time and space. It entails and requires this balance in which things perfect themselves at the expense of other things. It is a logically necessary aspect of a material universe that there is both growth and decay in different things at different times and in interaction with each other. These are not just side-effects but necessary consequences. Let me stress here that we are talking about natural evil: we shall see that this entailment does not apply in the case of moral evil.

What about God in all this? Well, as regards natural evil, we can legitimately say that God is its indirect cause since he has created a material universe. Now it may be objected: could not God have made the world in such a way that there are only good, growing things without any of the bad, decaying things? Well, the answer is no. To say this is not to impugn God's omnipotence. God could no more create a material universe in time and space without the balance of decay and growth and without the natural interaction of everything in an ordered world governed by its own natural laws than he could create a square circle or a married bachelor. The problem is not with God but with our question: the question contains a logical contradiction.

But now it may be objected on an apparently more fundamental level: why has God made a material universe at all if it entails all this? Here we need to pause. The question sounds sensible, but is it? It sounds as if one is asking a perfectly straightforward question: namely, why has God created a bad universe? But to ask why has God created a material universe, as opposed to any other kind, is equivalent to asking why has God created at all? And that is a decidedly odd question. For one thing, it presupposes that we have something with which we can compare this creation, a range of viable alternatives to be evaluated. But this is a nonsense. Creation is precisely everything that exists. Again, it raises all kinds of impossible, that is, incoherent, questions about the nature of 'creating', all of which presuppose that we are familiar with the kind of activity 'creating' is.

Of course, we know what we mean when we speak of 'creating' a work of art or a piece of furniture or a fuss. But to use the word literally, that is of God, is not to describe an activity but to assert a fact, the most basic fact there is: namely, that everything that exists depends on God for its continuing existence. God creates 'from nothing'. The very possibility of anything at all is also dependent on God for its existence. Talk of creating well or badly or inefficiently is, for these reasons, incoherent. To ask why God has created a material universe, as opposed to any other kind, is to ignore this incoherence.

But there's another reason why this question cannot make sense. What would a non-material universe entail? We don't know, but what we can say is that in asking for a non-material universe, we would be rejecting a natural world, governed by predictable natural laws, according to a rational and intelligible order and structure. In other words, we would be forfeiting a world susceptible of scientific investigation, a world knowable and manipulable by human beings for their benefit. In its place one would have, at the very least, an unpredictable, random world, disordered and dangerous, without any possibility of improvement or reasoned change. What kind of preferable chaos would this be?

Further, since matter is the principle of individuation – we are discrete individuals because we are material with physical boundaries – a non-material world would be a world without individuals. Since the objection was aimed at improving things for individuals, it seems to have cancelled itself out. It turns out to be a plea for non-existence.

But now we turn to moral evil, or evil done, or sin: the evil that is constituted by acts of human beings. Now here we can easily get distracted from the real question. While it is quite true that I may do something whose effects on others constitute natural evil or evil suffered, this is not the essence of the action but an effect. When we speak of moral evil, we are trying to focus attention not on the significance of the consequences of a given action, terrible as these may be – and this is covered in what we have said about natural evil – but on the significance of this free action in itself, that is for the one performing it.

Straightaway, let us say that what we said at the beginning about the meaning of the word 'evil' applies here too. The view that evil refers to a lack or deficiency applies equally to inanimate objects, animate non-human things and human beings alike. Of course, in the case of human beings the matter is infinitely more complicated. The question of what a human being is and, therefore, of what it is to be a good human being is obviously not as simple as what makes a desk a good desk or a book a good book. But, in principle, it is the same kind of account. A bad human being is one who lacks something that should be there, something, in other words, essential to his nature.

Other parts of the account we have so far given of natural evil, however, do not apply. For instance, the material universe argument does not apply when we are thinking of choices of the will. It is most definitely not inconsistent with the idea of a material universe that there should be people who make only good choices. Unlike natural evil, moral evil is not necessarily connected always to a good – except the good which is the existence of the person choosing wrongly. It may be, of course, that some good comes out of an evil deed: but this is not a necessary concomitant of the evil deed but only incidental. On the other hand, it may be that God brings good out of evil – and certainly we believe he does – but that is not accessible to reason alone: it is something we know only by faith.

Again, we must ask ourselves what it is, strictly speaking, we are referring to when we speak of moral evil. Clearly it is a deficiency in the form of failure: that is a failure to do something. Instead, I do something else in its place. It may be a positive thing, a good in the sense of a positive and existent goal or aim. But it is an inappropriate goal or end which, in the nature of things, displaces another, appropriate end or goal. What makes us speak of it as moral evil or sin is that it entails a failure to do what should be done and it is our knowledge of what is *not* being done that makes us speak of the evil in an action.

So the deficiency in moral evil is a failing to be in my actions what I am by nature. The failure consists in not doing those things which truly fulfil my nature: just like a washing machine that shredded rather than washed my clothes. As such, the real evil of moral evil or sin is the harm done to the perpetrator; it is his or her own nature and being that is diminished in the action. 'The action may be morally wrong because it does harm to others, but what we *mean* by saying that it is morally wrong is that it damages the perpetrator.'[16] The evil of the action, strictly speaking, is the diminution of our humanity. In other words, in a phrase that has become fashionable, we have failed to be fully human.

As such, the evil of moral evil is self-inflicted. Of course, the action I perform may have effects on someone else: for them this will be an evil, but evil suffered or natural evil. But it could be that they suffer the same evil as a result of a natural event, unconnected with a moral action. A gun, for instance, may be fired accidentally. The evil for the one who is hit is the same as if the gun had been discharged intentionally, but the question of moral evil involved is entirely different in these two cases. Or one can do a moral wrong in which there are no bad external effects on anybody else but the doer.

So, despite the apparent strangeness of this conclusion, what makes moral evil what it is, strictly speaking, is not its effects on others, but the fact that it damages or diminishes the doer. And here the damage done to the doer *is* the action, not an effect of the action. The action and the damage are the defect in the doer, even if good effects may incidentally follow.

The question will now be asked: what is God's role in all this? We saw that as far as natural evil is concerned we can reasonably say that, in so far as God brings about the good in which natural evil is rooted, he is its indirect cause. But what of moral evil; can he be said to be the cause of this? Now there is one way of answering this question which, despite its venerable pedigree, even among Christian thinkers, will not do. In their anxiety to defend God by removing the slightest suggestion that he causes evil, some theologians, beginning with St Augustine and right up to some contemporary writers, have argued that moral evil is wholly attributable to the exercise of free will. It is therefore nothing whatever to do with God because free actions are, according to this view, by definition, independent of God.

Now this argument, known as the Free Will Defence, makes some important points. We *are* responsible for our actions. But the Free Will Defence is nevertheless a seriously flawed argument. In fact, it does not and cannot get God off the hook for a very simple reason. It cannot be said, and this is what would have to be said for the argument to work, that God has no causal role in my free actions. On the contrary, as creator and sustainer of all that exists and has reality, God has an intimate causal role in all actions and events, more intimate indeed than our own causal role. God is the sustaining primary cause of everything that has existence, including actions, which also have existence. In fact, more than any of my other actions, my *free* actions especially manifest God's role as primary cause, since free actions are, by definition, *my* actions, and it is due to God's causality that I am me: God, in other words, is the cause of my causality.

Admittedly this is a difficult point. If you said of any other agent that he or she had a causal role in your actions, it would entail that you were not acting freely. But when this is said of God it has no such implication. Rather, it follows from his creative causing and sustaining of each person and a person's action and, *a fortiori*, a person's *free* actions since these are most explicitly one's own actions. In denying that the Free Will Defence works we are simply saying that whatever free actions are, they are not actions which are independent of God's causality. But this doesn't make them any less one's own actions.

So if the Free Will Defence doesn't explain how God is not the cause of moral evil or evil actions, where do we go from here? Remember we said that what we *mean* when we speak of moral as opposed to natural evil is a failure to do x where, instead, we do y. The evil is in the failure, that is in the absence of x. Now an absence is not an existing thing. What accounts for the absence in this case is the presence of another thing. The evil is the displacement of the true good by an attractive but ultimately frustrating, because inappropriate and therefore non-fulfilling, goal. In doing evil I choose between real and existing options: between what will genuinely fulfil me as a human being and some other goal which, in offering some partial and temporary fulfilment, conflicts with true fulfilment. When I choose evil I am failing to choose true happiness. The question of what causes the evil, beyond the simple observation that it consists in the presence of something else which I have chosen, does not arise. I am the cause of my own choice and God permits this choice. Indeed, without his allowing it by being its primary cause it could not happen.

We have now come full circle. We started from the fact that God permits evil, but we cannot know why. We cannot give a reason in the way we might give a reason for our own actions. He is his own reason. We cannot speak of God having reasons, just as we cannot speak of him having qualities: he is his qualities.

But now it may be objected: if God *could* have prevented moral evil, surely he *should* have: indeed, couldn't it be said that he was obliged to? Like the Free Will Defence, the argument based on God's obligations has some plausibility. But, on reflection, it will be apparent that God cannot be said to have obligations, as such. For one thing, only moral agents have obligations and God cannot be thought of as a moral agent.

Consider what we mean by a moral agent. Whatever else we mean, we mean an agent who exists in a given context due to which and derived from which he has some definite and specifiable responsibilities to those around him. It can be said that there are therefore expectations of him which can be legitimately entertained, and these expectations relate to his nature and its fulfilment. But can any of this be said, strictly speaking, of God? The answer is surely, no. God does not exist in any context; as Creator, he is the Creator of all possible contexts and the Creator of the very possibility of any context at all. If he cannot be said to exist in a context, he cannot be said to have obligations and responsibilities; nor can he be said to be the subject of expectations based on the possible fulfilment of his nature. On the contrary, he is the source of existence itself and is wholly what he is: his nature is wholly fulfilled. And he is the source of every context and therefore of all the responsibilities and obligations derived from them. If God is the Creator of everything – and within the Judaeo-Christian tradition this is the primary meaning of the word 'God' – then whatever else can be said about God it must be said that he transcends everything. And it follows that certain things we may say about some or all other things cannot be said of God.

Finally, many of the things which I have argued cannot be said are things that we *feel* should be said. Feelings are important. But sometimes we have to resist feelings and pursue reasons as carefully as we can. Our feelings in this case are, I suggest, based on a false assumption concerning God: namely, that he can be understood and judged and spoken of in the same way as any object within our experience. But this is to fall into anthropomorphism. The notion of evaluating what God does or is, is unintelligible. God does what he does and is what he is. Against what set of expectations would we measure the source of all expectations? God transcends any reason for acting, other than himself. What he is *is* his reason for acting as he does. And this is precisely what we cannot know.

So far I've tried to meet the challenge posed by the philosophical problem of evil on its own terms. Our conclusion has been a negative one: there are no good grounds for saying that the existence of evil counts against the existence of a good God. Arguments, however, will take us only so far. The practical problem of evil still remains untouched. So now we must consider what light is shed on this problem by Christian faith.

First, Christian faith does nothing to circumvent or dispel or short circuit the fact of evil, especially in its form as sin. Sin and suffering are as much a mystery for the Christian as for anyone else, and just as painful in the experiencing. Nor is it any part of genuine Christian faith to try to render evil palatable or explicable or justifiable in terms of reasons God might have for permitting evil. This is what many well-meaning theodicists attempt. On the contrary, is it not obscene and morally repugnant to try to rationalize evil by thinking of it as somehow worthwhile 'in the long term'.

If Christianity sheds any light on the mystery of evil, it will not take the form of theological arguments and formulae. Rather, it will consist in reminding us of what it is that we place our faith in. Christianity's answer is to direct our gaze to the Cross of Christ which confronts us with the ultimate mystery of all existence. Here we face squarely all the seemingly irreconcilable contradictions of human experience. Paradoxically, it is in the Cross that the problem of evil is most clearly manifest, for here, contrary to the view that God must be indifferent to our suffering, he becomes the victim of evil in order to overcome, on our behalf, the evil we have inflicted on him. In this we see the mystery of infinite love which is the only thing that can answer the mystery of evil. But in this demonstration of love we are made to face the hard truth about ourselves. Though we would rather not look, we are shown both what we have made of ourselves without God: namely, sinful and self-destructive; and what we are meant to be with him: namely, human and vital. In the Cross, the polar possibilities of sinful humanity and true humanity, evil and love, are juxtaposed for our contemplation and instruction, but only by God's becoming the victim of evil himself. By suffering with us, Christ shows us that *we* are the victims of our sins. But by dying on the Cross Christ breaks the infernal circle whereby we, the victims, go on to become in our turn victimizers. Christ in himself ends this perpetual cycle of evil.

What God would be credible who stood aloof from and showed no solidarity with suffering? And yet, nobody could invent such a God who becomes a victim alongside us. We could never risk identifying a mere projection of our minds with what is most painful and difficult to bear in human life. And yet, in the suffering of Christ, the mystery of evil is left intact – indeed it is deepened, precisely by being set alongside the even greater mystery of love. Of course, as in all love, we are left to draw our conclusion – freely – without the constraint of argument.

If we cannot understand why God permits evil, it is because we cannot understand what it is to be God. For the answer *is* God and God transcends all understanding, making himself known in the ultimate human mystery of love. The problem of evil is in our understanding and language, not in God.

THE CHURCH: DO WE NEED IT?

We live in a culture that is suspicious of institutions and their claims. We fear, not without justification, that they will limit our freedom and self-expression. Individualism is a pervasive and, to our generation, self-evident good.

But it is not an unalloyed good. Loss of communal identity and a sense of place and roots are main contributing factors to a felt dis-ease within society and to many of its problems. As with everything, it is a question of balance between the claims and needs of both communal and individual well-being, between which there must be a mutually beneficial coexistence.

I mention all this because the Catholic Church is often feared as an oppressive institution and resented for telling people what to believe. Many within the Church question its authority to say what the Christian faith is and to say how we should put this faith into practice. So it is a pressing necessity to be clear about the nature of the Church, its meaning, and the source of its life and authority.

The heart of Christianity is a person, not a book or an institution or a set of rules. The most important fact of the Church's existence is that it was founded by Jesus as an instrument of his mission of reconciliation and redemption. He is the source of its life, not just in the beginning but throughout its existence. If this fundamental fact is not true then the whole thing is a shameful and destructive sham.

The Church, however, is not just another human institution founded by a particular individual at some point in the distant past. In a sense that must exceed our understanding, it is the Body of Christ in the world, the continuing presence of Jesus Christ, the Son of God.

But who belongs to the Church? The answer is simple: all those baptized, since baptism incorporates – the word is exactly the right one – a person into the Body of Christ. But this assertion needs to be nuanced in order to make clear how the baptized stand in relation to, first, the unbaptized and second, among themselves. The way to do this is to find a way of explicating the nature of the Church in broader terms.

God is the mystery which is the source and ground of existence: the Creator, in other words. We have seen that this is not the facile assertion that it appears to be when confused with the assertions of scientific cosmologists interested, as we all are, in the processes that give rise to the kind of physical world we know. Creation in the fundamental sense of God's creation of the universe, is not a process or a coming to be of one state of affairs from another antecedent state of affairs. That something is created means that it is dependent for its very existence on God, at all points in its existence and not just at the beginning.

This ineffable and incomprehensible God makes himself known, and makes his love for what he has created known, in the person of Christ, the second person of the Blessed Trinity, God made man, Jesus of Nazareth, who was born, lived and died a fully human life in our history at a definite point in concrete circumstances.

Christ is therefore the sacrament, the manifestation of God and his saving love. The work of Christ is the work of God, redeeming and reconciling, saving and forgiving, and restoring us to life by sharing his own life with us. In other words, Christ is the sacrament of God, the effective presence of God within his creation.

And the Church is the continuing explicit and effective presence of Christ in this world. It is, therefore, in the words of the Second Vatican Council, the 'sacrament or instrumental sign of intimate union with God and the unity of all humanity.' (*Lumen Gentium1*, in Tanner, vol. 2, p. 849). The purpose of Christ's coming among us is precisely to unite us to God, and to unite us among ourselves. The Church is the living sign and effective means of this unity and communion.

A further level of this sacramentality, so to speak, is in the seven sacraments of the Church, which are the manifestation of God's love for us, some at particular points in our lives and for particular important purposes, others as permanent accompaniments throughout our lives. In these sacred actions God's saving work is accomplished in us. In the sacraments God both shows us what he does for us and he does what he shows.

Now everything that is true of the Church, everything that pertains to its essence, its nature, derives from this understanding and reality. The problem is to distinguish between the essential and the accidental.

How does the Church come about, in practice? Jesus gathered about him actual individuals and taught them by word and example. His teaching, which encompasses what we need for our salvation, has been handed down through successive generations of the Church into our own day. Hence the prominence in Catholicism (and now in much secular post-modern thought) of the word 'tradition'. The essential message of this teaching that has been handed down is, of course, simple: we have been reconciled with God in Christ and this has been achieved through the life and saving death of Christ, the manifestation of God's love for his creation. How is this teaching preserved and handed on?

Christ did not abandon the Church he had founded. He spoke of sending the Holy Spirit, the Paraclete, the Advocate, who would inspire and guide the Church into all truth. It is the Spirit which ensures the Church's unity and adherence to the true faith. The Church was to grow in its understanding of what Jesus had taught, which is why doctrines may be argued over and give rise to new, more adequate formulations of what is an unchanging faith. Hence the notion of 'development of doctrine' which was of such especial interest to John Henry Newman, who actually converted to Catholicism while writing his own work on the idea in 1845. But the idea has a long pedigree. A much earlier writer, St Vincent of Lérins (d. 450), tried to explain how a doctrine can develop and yet remain the same doctrine by citing the example of the continuing identity that persists in the same human individual between childhood and adulthood.

The notion of development of doctrine has often been regarded with scepticism if not cynicism by many outside the Catholic Church and some within. Such cynicism will be seen to be misplaced if one bears in mind salient aspects and principles of Christian belief already touched on: namely, that God is an unfathomable mystery and will always remain so; that Christianity is about the person of Jesus, who is God; that all doctrines and dogmas seek to point us in the direction of a truth that will always exceed our understanding; that all doctrine involves language that is, in principle, finite and provisional and therefore always incomplete and inadequate to the truth it seeks to articulate.

Finally, the Church has traditionally been spoken of under the four headings or characteristics mentioned in the Creed: one, holy, catholic and apostolic. The Church is undivided, as the Body of Christ is undivided. This might seem to be in flat contradiction to the empirical facts: after all, Christendom is manifestly divided. Now this raises an important issue and one which can be said to have distinguished Catholics from other Christians. The Church, in Catholic thought, is a divine institution. It is not, in other words, merely the aggregate of human individuals that make up its number. In saying that the Church is the Body of Christ, Catholics are saying that the Church results from the community established not just among themselves but between themselves and Christ. That Christendom is divided results from the lamentable failure of Christians to manifest and make visible this communal identity with Christ himself, which is the foundation of any community among themselves.

This same principle applies when Catholics speak of the Church as holy; its holiness is the holiness of Christ. Again, the holiness of the Church does nothing to guarantee automatically the personal holiness of its members. This much is apparent to even the most casual observer. All manner of vicious deeds have been done in the name of the Church and those charged with the grave responsiblities of service within the Church have often been the perpetrators. Widely reported instances of horrific crimes committed even by individuals occupying positions of responsibility and trust within the Church, albeit a tiny and unrepresentative minority, further confirm that the holiness of the Church coexists with the personal defectibility of its members.

Again, the Church is said in the Creed to be catholic, and by this it is asserted that the Church is not a sect or in any way limited to a particular culture or period of history. Though the Church began in a specific place and time among a particular group of Jews, it almost immediately emerged as essential to the Church's self-understanding that the message of salvation proclaimed by Jesus and preached by the Church was intended for all, without exception.

The last of the four credal characteristics of the Church binds together the other marks: the Church is apostolic. This has a twofold meaning: on the one hand it asserts that the Church is in living continuity with the followers chosen by Jesus himself, the apostles, and is therefore the Church Jesus founded. On the other hand it is intimately connected with the catholic nature of the Church: that is, its very *raison d'être* is to proclaim the message of salvation to all nations, without exception.

In the Orthodox liturgy, during the celebration of the Eucharist, it is said at one point that the sacred elements are 'holy things for holy people'. We, the 'holy people' are also sinners, suffering the same frailties and prone to the same failings as everybody else. And yet, the Christian believes that he is joined to and incorporated into Christ, who is the holy God. It is a lifelong and even longer work of grace to bring about harmony between the holiness that is Christ's and the holiness to which we are called.

THE SACRAMENTS: SAVING SIGNS OR MAGIC?

The theory and practice of the sacraments has always been one of the most conspicuous characteristics of Catholicism. One could justifiably say that the concept of sacrament is even more central in that the Second Vatican Council chose to speak of the Church itself as the sacrament of salvation. An adequate understanding of the seven sacraments, therefore, must begin from an understanding of the Church. Not surprisingly, the sacraments were the subject of controversy during the Protestant Reformation in Europe precisely because the nature and role of the Church was the central point of disagreement from which all the others arose.

But an adequate understanding of the sacraments and their importance in the lives of Catholics must also begin from an appreciation of the everyday aspects of our bodily existence and the role of gestures in the communication of our feelings and thoughts and the crucial formative place of language in constituting us as human beings.

Gestures both express and create that which gives rise to them. Language is not just a sophisticated means of communicating information: bees and other creatures have equally effective means of doing that. What makes language so vital to human beings is that among the many other things it does it communicates meaning: through language, in other words, we communicate ourselves.

Language is one of the greatest mysteries of human existence, a reflection, indeed, of the mystery of human life itself. We do things with words: we greet, question, command, inform, beseech, excite, terrify, offend, abuse, insult, promise, break promises, break hearts, encourage, intimidate, forgive, flatter, let off steam, get married.

Such communication and shaping of our lives takes place not just in words but in gestures and signs that are always revealing of ourselves, no matter how we may use them to conceal. A smile is a good example. But what these means of communication have in common is that they involve our bodies and that they belong to and can only be understood within a shared way of life. Out of context they are meaningless.

Now I have said from the beginning that Catholicism claims to be a reasonable belief. It takes for granted the fact that our minds and our reason are vital in the conduct of our lives and in the understanding of our faith. It has always held that we can come to the conviction by reason alone; that there exists something which accounts for the existence of the universe. This, however, is necessary but not sufficient for Christian faith. Christianity is rooted in the conviction not only that God has made us but that he has spoken to us, drawn near to us, and offered us the possibility of communion with him by sharing his life with us. This we could never come to know by reason alone.

In order to speak to us God must enter into the context which alone makes communication possible. All human communication is bodily communication. Thus he speaks to us in the Incarnation by which he enters into human history as one of us. And he has only one thing to say to us, one thing to communicate: himself. And he is love. And as lovers seek above all else to share their lives with each other, so God seeks to share his life with us by enabling us to share in his life. This is what is meant by the life of grace.

'In many and various ways, God spoke to our fathers by the prophets: but in these last days he has spoken to us by his Son.' In this stark statement by the author of the letter to the Hebrews the sacramental principle is enunciated. Namely, the material, earthly realities of our embodied, creaturely existence can be the vehicles of the divine in our midst. God, in other words, uses human language to communicate himself to us, to offer himself in friendship. Jesus is the sacrament of God: all that he does and says carries divine significance. And it is the humanity of Jesus that is the vehicle of divinity. The Church is the sacrament of the salvation Jesus makes possible, a salvation that consists in sharing God's life, living in the communion of friendship with him. In time and space and encompassing the material realities of our earthly, embodied life, the Church continues to make visible and accessible through perceptible signs the presence of God, in the person of Christ, to the world.

In the life of the Church and of each individual Catholic the seven sacraments are the explicit ('explicit' because his presence is not limited to the sacraments) moments of Christ's presence in which he communicates himself to us and we are enabled to respond in love to him. Some of these sacraments happen only once and take place at crucial points in a person's life; others accompany us through life, reaffirming and making real his presence throughout our journey. But the goal of each of the sacraments is the same goal as that which belongs to the Church as such and which is the purpose of the Incarnation: namely, communion with God, sharing his life.

Magical rituals generally aim to invoke and make present a force or deity that is otherwise absent. In the sacraments, it is the presence of God which is the very ground of existence that is made explicit. Far from manipulating creation and fracturing its order in the pursuit of extraordinary goals and objectives, God's saving work is accomplished in us through the sacraments precisely by revealing to us what is already there as the foundation of our lives: namely, God.

In these sacred actions God shows us what he does for us and he does what he shows. Thus in each of the sacraments there is a coming together of word, gesture and matter: the three elements of human communication. To take two of them, there are, for example, in baptism the words in the name of the Father, the Son and the Holy Spirit. There is the action of cleansing either by pouring or immersion. And there is the matter which is water, symbolic of the effects of this particular sacrament: the washing clean which makes possible the incorporation of the individual into the Church, the Body of Christ. And in the Eucharist there are the words of institution: this is my Body given up for you, this is my Blood poured out for you. There is the gesture of sharing a meal. And there is the matter of the sacrament, namely, food and drink, bread and wine. Thus, given the appropriate dispositions of those participating, that communion of life and love between us and God for which Christ became man is made real.

Of the seven sacraments, the Holy Eucharist, or the Mass (in the East it is called 'The Divine Liturgy') is accorded special importance. The Second Vatican Council speaks of it as 'the source and culmination of all Christian life' – *totius vitae christianae fontem et culmen (Lumen Gentium 1,* in Tanner, vol. 2, p. 857). The sharing of God's life, which is the goal and purpose of all the sacraments, and of the Christian life as a whole, is nowhere as explicitly realized as in the Mass and Holy Communion.

In the past, before the by no means universal but growing convergence of Christian belief and practice, the Eucharist was at the centre of controversy. During the Reformation debates, the parties in dispute were characterizable, among other things by their divergent understandings of the Eucharist. The key elements debated were the idea of sacrifice associated with the Mass as in the phrase 'the sacrifice of the Mass' and the notion of Christ's 'Real Presence'. It must be said also that, among non-Christians, nowhere more than in the Catholic understanding of the Eucharist are the sacraments open to the misunderstanding that they involve something akin to magic.

The Mass is spoken of, within the rite itself and in the teaching of the Church, as sacrificial but, at times, even Catholics have misunderstood what this means and have contributed to misunderstanding on the part of other Christians and those outside Christianity. The Mass is the sacrifice of Christ, offered once and for all, on Calvary. This act of God made man is unique. What happens in the Mass is not a new sacrifice, not even a replay, as it were, of Christ's sacrifice. Rather his unique sacrifice, his act of selfless love in freely accepting his death on our behalf, is made present sacramentally in time so that in the historical unfolding of our lives we are enabled to participate in the one sacrifice of Calvary. The Eucharist is not a substitute for his sacrifice, nor does it add to it or happen alongside it. And Christ does not die again. At Mass we are in the presence of Christ and his outpouring of love for all mankind. In a real sense, all time, past and future, is gathered in the present at Mass. At the same time the Eucharist looks to the future and the fullness of communion with Christ which is begun and daily renewed in this sacrament. Some verses from T. S. Eliot touch this timeless sense of the eucharistic sacrifice:

> **At the still point of the turning world. Neither flesh nor fleshless;**
> **Neither from nor towards; at the still point, there the dance is,**
> **But neither arrest nor movement. And do not call it fixity,**
> **Where past and future are gathered. Neither movement from nor**
> **towards,**
> **Neither ascent nor decline. Except for the point, the still point,**
> **There would be no dance, and there is only the dance.**
>
> *Burnt Norton*

The other point of controversy in eucharistic doctrine concerns the presence of Christ in the sacrament. This is spoken of in Catholic teaching as the Real Presence. 'Real' here does not mean 'authentic' but comes from the Latin *in re,* in the thing itself, namely, the species of bread and wine. Traditionally, the word 'transubstantiation' has been used to describe the nature of the change that takes place during the Mass through which Christ becomes present under the form of bread and wine. But belief in the Real Presence of Christ is part of the Apostolic Tradition. It is nothing new, even if for a long period of time the Church had no single and defined way of articulating its belief. As early as the second century, Justin Martyr (100–65) writes:

> **As Jesus Christ our Saviour, being incarnate by God's word, took flesh and blood for our salvation, so also we have been taught that the food consecrated by the word of prayer which comes from him, from which our flesh and blood are nourished by transformation, is the flesh and blood of that incarnate Jesus.**
>
> *(First Apology lxvi, 2)*

And Cyril of Jerusalem (315–87) says:

> **What seems bread, is not bread, even if it seems such to the taste, but the body of Christ, and what seems wine is not wine, even though it has its taste, but the blood of Christ.**
>
> *(Catecheses 4,9)*

The word 'transubstantiation' came into official use in the thirteenth century at the Fourth Lateran Council in 1215. But it had been used in earlier debates to express what the Church believed about the eucharistic presence, e.g. by Gregory VII in the oath signed by Berengarius of Tours (1010–88), after the intervention of the great Archbishop of Canterbury, Lanfranc of Bec (1010–89).

The Lateran Council's statement is unequivocal:

> **His body and blood are truly contained in the sacrament of the altar under the forms of bread and wine, the bread and wine having been changed in substance, by God's power, into his body and blood, so that in order to achieve this mystery of unity we receive from God what he received from us.**
>
> *(Lateran IV cap 1: On the Catholic Faith, in Tanner vol. 1, p. 230)*

The notion of 'transubstantiation' entered into the definition of the mode of Christ's presence in the Eucharist at the Council of Trent in the sixteenth century and the statement of the Council of Trent is equally unambiguous:

> . . . the holy council teaches and openly and without qualifica-
> tion professes that after the consecration of the bread and wine,
> our Lord Jesus Christ, true God and true man, is truly, really and
> substantially contained in the propitious sacrament of the holy
> eucharist under the appearance of those things which are per-
> ceptible to the senses. Nor are the two assertions incompatible,
> that our Saviour is ever seated in heaven at the right hand of the
> Father in his natural mode of existing, and that he is neverthe-
> less sacramentally present to us by his substance in many other
> places in a mode of existing which, though we can hardly
> express it in words, we can grasp with minds enlightened by
> faith as possible to God and most firmly believe . . .
>
> *(Decree on the most holy sacrament of the eucharist, cap 1, in*
> Tanner vol. 2, pp. 693–4.)

And

> . . . by the consecration of the bread and wine, there takes place
> the change of the whole substance of the bread into the sub-
> stance of the body of Christ our Lord, and the whole substance of
> the wine into the substance of the blood and the holy catholic
> church has suitably and properly called this change transubstan-
> tiation.
>
> *(cap 4, in Tanner vol. 2, p. 695)*

Catholics are committed to the teaching of both the Fourth
Lateran Council and the Council of Trent. And the teaching is
clear. What is meant by 'substance' in these statements is what a
thing is. And both these statements presuppose that how a thing
appears, its extrinsic qualities, are not part of its substance, since
they can change over time. But in so far as this teaching could,
conceivably, be expressed by means of other terminology, then
other terms could be acceptable. Catholic teaching on the
eucharistic presence is that what is received under the outward
forms of bread and wine is the whole Christ, not just his body or
just his blood. Traditionally, this was expressed as his body,
blood, soul and divinity. The outward forms of bread and wine
of course symbolize nourishment. But it is Christ, the bread from

heaven, who is this nourishment. And it is communion with the whole Christ that is effected by receiving the consecrated elements. But this is a work of grace, not a mechanical transaction. There is no inward communion without the appropriate dispositions, principally the desire for such communion.

Even in the early days of the Church, misunderstandings of the Eucharist abounded among its opponents. Most tellingly, the charge of cannibalism was levelled at Christians. This arose from straightforward misapprehension of what was heard. But even among Catholics, especially in the early Middle Ages, certain distortions of eucharistic doctrine gained currency, notably among those who adopted an extreme realist position.

But Catholic teaching is clear: in the sacrament of the Eucharist, a change takes place such that the reality of the bread gives place to the reality of the body of Christ. Christ is not physically present in the same way that other people are present: but he is personally present. When the host is broken, Christ is not broken. When we eat the host, we receive Christ, but Christ is not chewed or broken down by our digestive juices. Indeed, Christ does not cease to be in heaven when he is made present at the Eucharist.

Nowhere is the teaching of the Catholic Church about the Holy Eucharist summed up more succinctly than in the anthem written *c.* 1263 by St Thomas Aquinas for the Feast of Corpus Christi:

> **This is a Holy Banquet indeed, in which Christ Himself is made our food, the memory of his Passion is told again, grace fills the mind and heart and there is given to us an assurance of the glory that one day will be ours.**

OUR LADY: MARIOLOGY OR MARIOLATRY?

The church of Santa Maria in Trastevere stands on the site of one of the oldest churches in Rome and the first to be dedicated to Mary, the mother of Jesus, in the mid-fourth century. The present church results from a rebuilding in the mid-twelfth century. There are many objects and works of art of outstanding beauty in Santa Maria in Trastevere, but the mosaics, practically all depicting the Virgin, are not only some of the finest in Rome: they also say in pictorial form, more than any doctrinal formulation can express, why Mary occupies the unique place she has in the Catholic faith.

The mosaic in the apsidal semi-dome is the earliest known portrayal of Mother and Son, seated together on two thrones. The majestic figure of Christ is reminiscent of the Pantocrator figure of Byzantium, while the virgin Mary, his mother, is depicted as an Empress. But there is a rarely noticed detail in the work which departs entirely from the formal, rather stiff scene of regal splendour: Christ has his arm around the shoulder of his mother, in a gesture of filial affection and familiarity.

More than any other image this sets the context for understanding the teaching of the Catholic Church from the earliest times concerning Mary. All that can be said and all that is taught about Mary arises from and is rooted in her relationship with Jesus, and Catholic understanding of her role and place emerges alongside the evolution of our understanding of Christ's person and nature. Indeed, much of what soon came to be taken for granted about Mary by Catholics was not developed separately, in a effort to extol her or heap further honours upon her, but rather as a corollary to a fuller and more comprehensive understanding of the Incarnation.

All this can be seen most clearly in the earliest and most important formulation of faith concerning Mary: namely, the assertion, first officially articulated at the Council of Ephesus in 431, but going back as early as Origen of Alexandria (c. 185–254), that Mary is the Mother of God. This official doctrine of faith is spoken of by the present pope as 'a seal upon the dogma of the Incarnation' (*Redemptoris Mater* n. 4). It is primarily, in other words, a doctrine about Christ, and only secondarily about his mother. Indeed, the title in Greek, *theotokos*, literally 'God-bearer', was promulgated at the Council precisely in response to the views of Nestorius, the Patriarch of Constantinople, who held that in Jesus there were two persons: the man whom Mary gave birth to, and the Son of God. By implication, Mary was therefore the mother of the man Jesus but not the mother of God. The Council declared this view heretical and defended the traditional view that Jesus is truly the Son of God, the Word made flesh: he is both human and divine. The assertion that Mary is *theotokos* was a corollary to this view. The Second Vatican Council stressed that devotion to Mary is intended to lead to Christ and that whatever is said of her refers to him, 'the origin of all truth, holiness and piety' (*Lumen Gentium* n. 67 Tanner Vol.2, p.897.)

It is true that devotion to Mary has taken forms at certain times and in certain places that have understandably created the impression that she is more than human and the object of worship rather than deserving of devotion and reverence. As a result, it has seemed to many outside the Church that devotion to Mary bordered on idolatry. The Catholic Church in the Second Vatican Council showed sensitivity to this problem and sought to avoid anything that might continue to give this impression. 'Let them carefully refrain from whatever might by word or deed lead the separated brethren or any others whatsoever into error about the true doctrine of the Church.' To this end, the Council chose not to devote a separate document to the subject of Mary, as some of the more conservative Council Fathers had suggested. Instead, a single chapter in a much larger document on the nature of the Church was given over to the topic, thus reinforcing the more traditional understanding that Mary does not stand over against and alongside the Church and the person of Christ, but has her place as a member of the Church, one of the faithful. She is a human being, indeed she is the most fully human member of the Church, unique in her faithful response to God and thus unique in holiness.

This uniqueness is the background to the two doctrines concerning Mary that, along with her perpetual virginity, have been controversial outside the Catholic Church, among both other Christians and non-Christians: namely, the Immaculate Conception promulgated in 1854 and the Assumption in 1950. The dogma of the Immaculate Conception states that Mary 'was, from the first moment of her conception, by the singular grace and privilege of almighty God and in view of the merits of Jesus Christ the Saviour of the human race, preserved free from all stain of original sin'. (Notice that this is entirely different from, though often confused with, the doctrine that Jesus was conceived without the intervention of a human father: his, in other words, was a virginal conception.) Although the dogma was defined only in 1854 by Pius IX, the feast goes back at least to the seventh century. And though it appears explicitly nowhere in the Scriptures several passages have always been understood to point towards it.

The background to this teaching is the doctrine of original

sin. It is claimed that Mary uniquely was untouched by sin, even that tendency to sin in which all human beings share as a result of the Fall. But the teaching was not universally accepted in the Middle Ages. Significant figures such as St Anselm (d. 1109), St Bernard (d. 1153), St Thomas Aquinas (d. 1274) and St Bonaventure (d. 1274) disagreed with the doctrine, arguing that it removed Mary from the human race by suggesting that she was not in need of salvation through Christ's redemptive work. But it was another Franciscan, Duns Scotus (d. 1308) who argued that Mary was indeed redeemed by Christ, but rather than being rescued from original sin, as we are, she was preserved from it. Her being conceived without sin is thus as much, if not a more explicit result of Christ's redemptive power. It is fitting, he argued, that such a grace should be given to the one who was to bear the Son of God, so that her redemption was anticipated. In practice, this means that she lived in perfect communion with God from the first instant of her existence. The reign of sin, in other words, came to an end in her and the ultimate destiny of us all is seen luminously in the life of Mary, 'full of grace'. The English historian and theologian, Eadmer, a member of St Anselm's household and a constant companion when Anselm was Archbishop of Canterbury, expressed the matter with pithy succinctness in the first systematic work on the doctrine, his *Tractatus de conceptione S. Mariae*: He says there '*Potuit, decuit, fecit*'. 'God could have done it, it was fitting that he should, and therefore he did do it.'

As Mary's birth was exceptional so for the same reasons was her death. Though the doctrine of Mary's Assumption was promulgated only in 1950 by Pius XII, belief that Mary was taken body and soul into heaven first appeared in the sixth century. The view that Mary's body did not corrupt in the grave but was immediately reunited with her soul was common from around the beginning of the fifth century. Belief in the corporal assumption of Mary has been prominent and widespread in Eastern Christianity from the earliest times, where it is known as the Dormition, the Falling Asleep of the Blessed Virgin Mary.

The thrust of this doctrine is that, as Mary benefited from and received the fruits of the redemptive work of her Son by anticipation, so she shares already in the fullness of his resurrection. And as the resurrection of Christ itself asserts, among much else, the essential unity of body and soul in human nature, so Mary's assumption, 'body and soul', also stresses that the whole person is saved and redeemed. Falsely spiritual views of human nature, in which the emphasis is placed on the soul at the expense of denigrating the body, are thus set aside.

The formulation of the doctrine takes no position on the disputed question of whether or not Mary actually died. The teaching is consistent with either view. Its central significance, as with all doctrines concerning Mary, is its relationship to and dependence on the saving action of Christ in restoring humanity to the fullness of the destiny for which we have been created. So the Second Vatican Council could say that 'the mother of Jesus, as already glorified in body and soul in heaven . . . is the image and the beginning of the Church which will receive fulfilment in the age that is to come . . . here on earth until the day of the Lord arrives she shines forth as a sign of sure hope and comfort for the pilgrim people of God' (*Lumen Gentium* n. 68 Tanner Vol.2, p.898).

No less a figure than Carl Jung spoke of the definition of the dogma in 1950 as the most significant religious event for 500 years. He saw in it the restoration of the much-needed feminine principle in a world increasingly dominated by materialist and technological philistinism.

There is now much writing about Mary from a feminist perspective. The chief value of such work is as a corrective to the view of Mary that predominated in the past, in which her humanity was subordinated to her exalted role as Mother of God. But no amount of doctrinal formulation and elaboration should be allowed to obscure the fact that Mary was a poor Jewish girl in first-century Palestine. The full flourishing of her womanly human nature can therefore be a source of inspiration and encouragement not only to women but to all members of the Church. In Mary, precisely those characteristics and values that are indispensable conditions for the healthy and wholesome flourishing of any human person and for society as a whole, are given prominence in the Church for the good of the world.

THE PAPACY: HELP OR OBSTACLE?

The convergence in matters of belief and practice between different Christian denominations, though far from complete, cannot but be marvelled at by anybody over the age of 35. Over the last 25 years undreamed of developments have taken place and, with notable exceptions, shaped by political as much as by genuinely religious considerations, the cessation of stifled if not open hostility has provided an ecumenical context fruitful in ways unimaginable to previous generations.

The one issue, however, which still constitutes a logjam for many Christians who are not Roman Catholics is the papacy. And it is still the feature which distinguishes Catholics from all other Christians. In the same way, the difficulties many feel about the papacy are distilled in one aspect of the Catholic understanding of this office: namely, infallibility.

What is more, while papal infallibility is regarded by some Christians as an insuperable obstacle to the reunion of Christendom, it is also regarded by many others as an intolerable affront to the rights of human reason and self-governance, so cherished by modernity. The quotation which begins this essay was inspired in its original context by certain distorted views of papal infallibility adopted at the time of its promulgation by a small but influential number of Catholics, the Ultramontanes. This chapter describes the context of this much-debated aspect of Roman Catholicism in the hope of showing more clearly what was intended by the Fathers of the First Vatican Council who promulgated it in 1870 and how hedged-in this doctrine is by rarely referred to qualifications and nuances.

As with the papacy itself the doctrine of papal infallibility is an aspect of the Catholic understanding of the Church itself and its teaching role. The primary question to be asked, therefore, in pursuit of an appropriate understanding of infallibility, concerns the nature of revelation and the teaching of that revelation to succeeding generations.

I said earlier that Christianity is about the person of Christ and what he, uniquely, offers us for our salvation. Faith, therefore, does not have as its object any theological system or set of propositions, however hallowed; the object of faith is God alone, made known to us in his Word, Jesus Christ. Our salvation and redemption is secured not by intellectual assent to this or that proposition or by adherence to this or that institution, but in being united in the communion of love and friendship with him. The truth in which we put our hope is a person, not a formula.

Nevertheless, this does not obviate the need of words and doctrine: on the contrary, it presupposes and demands it because this conviction must be communicated, related to us as human beings, as users of language. No choice of language will ever be adequate or complete, but we have no choice but to avail ourselves of language in the effort to communicate the Gospel of salvation accurately. Christ himself used spoken human words to convey divine truth, and words are still central to the communication of divine truth.

The Church is Catholic in the sense of receiving the charge to proclaim its Good News to all, beyond the limitations of time, space and culture. Its Good News, of course, is the fact of Christ himself and the revelation of God in him. That revelation is complete in Christ, simply because he is God. There is nothing more to be added. But the Church's task is perennial, and precisely because it continues in time and extends in space, the presence of Christ its teaching role is part of its very essence.

It must be the case that this teaching role first bequeathed to the apostles and continued in the Church carries with it the authority of Christ himself; it cannot be otherwise because without it there would now be no Gospel or Good News of salvation or Church. But for this very reason the scope of this teaching authority is limited. As did the apostles, so the Church has the authority to teach only what Jesus himself taught. Its authority pertains only to handing on what was received from him. The early Church clearly recognized and acknowledged this. St Paul, for example, explicitly draws a clear distinction between what he thinks and what he has received from the Lord.

Now it follows that this authority must entail that the apostles' teaching of what the Lord gave us is infallible. Again, how could it be otherwise? It simply could not make sense to be given, on the one hand, authority to proclaim his message while lacking, on the other hand, the guarantee of inerrancy in conveying such teaching. And not only in conveying it but also in explicating and developing this teaching. This teaching role cannot be simply the rote repetition of formulae and words. That this cannot be the case is evident from consideration of the task set the Church, namely, to preach the Gospel to all nations. This necessarily involves interpretation and translation, restatement and application in order successfully to communicate the faith to peoples of other languages, times and cultures.

This teaching role did not disappear with the death of the apostles but was integral to the Church itself and continues as part of the Church's essence. How else could the Good News be handed on in vastly different situations? How else could the Gospel be received and made personal by succeeding generations except by drawing out implications and applications appropriate to new settings and needs and understood by new minds reflecting on the original message? And should we not expect this to be so simply from the fact that the truth handed on in the person of Christ is inexhaustible? How else could we be assured that what is taught is identical with and rooted in the original teaching, and not some new doctrine?

The exercise of the charism of infallibility does not involve any new revelation: its purpose is wholly contrary to this in that it is given to the Church in order that the teaching of Christ should be preserved from addition or change. That task of preservation does not, of course, mean setting it in aspic, as it were, but by means of a living tradition which is able to interpret and apply that teaching, to render it intelligible to new situations and new questions. The words and formulae used are just that: human attempts to give adequate expression to what is inexpressible. But they nevertheless point us in the direction of the truth even if they themselves, being human constructs, are always provisional and in need of further explication.

This, then, is the necessary context within which to understand the doctrine of papal infallibility. Catholics believe that one of the roles of the papacy is to be *one* of the organs of this infallible teaching authority of the Church. It is nothing other than the power to declare, when necessary, what is and what is not part of the Church's faith bequeathed to it by its Lord. In other words, Catholics believe that when the Church, through either the pope alone or the pope in union with all his fellow bishops, declares that such and such is of the Catholic faith, that it is revealed by God and to be held by all, then it is so. And in doing this the Church is merely explicating what has already been revealed by Christ. The Church cannot propose as dogmas anything not contained implicitly within the original revelation.

Notice the doctrine of papal infallibility does not imply an oracular understanding of the teaching authority of the Church. Nor does it involve the pope gazing into some crystal ball and circumventing the labour of understanding and reflection. Nor, again, does it mean that the doctrine of papal infallibility itself is not open to development, interpretation and application. It falls equally within the scope of that feature of doctrinal formulation which it undergirds.

The pope is a bishop, of Rome, and his office as pope arises from the primacy attaching to the see of the apostles Peter and Paul from the earliest times. As early as the second century, Ignatius of Antioch, writing to the Romans, speaks of Rome as 'pre-eminent in love' and 'teacher of others'. Many authors see this as the earliest recognition of papal primacy: as the focus of unity and charity and as the universal teacher of faith.

It must be said that positions have softened on all sides, including on the part of the papacy. Cordial meetings have taken place between the popes and the Patriarchs of Constantinople and between the popes and the Archbishops of Canterbury. The present pope has called for the help of other Church leaders in reappraising his own role and discerning the authentic tradition of papal authority. As recently as 1995 Pope John Paul II published an encyclical entitled *Ut Unum Sint – That They May All Be One* which is both a call for Christian unity and an invitation to enter into dialogue about those things which still hold Christians back from unity. Among these issues, the pope acknowledges the exercise of papal primacy as Bishop of Rome and he invites Church leaders 'to engage with me in a patient and fraternal dialogue in which, leaving useless controversies behind, we could listen to one another, keeping before us only the will of Christ for his Church'.

The difficulties mostly felt by non-Roman Catholics about the papacy have concerned the notion of jurisdiction, that is, the right to exercise judgement concerning what is appropriate. The Orthodox Churches of the East, for instance, refused in the eleventh century to accept the primacy of the Bishop of Rome, choosing to regard him as only a *primus inter pares*, first among equals. The Protestant Churches of the West in the sixteenth century rejected any role whatsoever for the pope. This call for help and dialogue implicitly recognizes that, though the papacy may belong to the essential constitution of the Church, the question of how this ministry is exercised is never answered once and for all. What is called for is a return to a form of Petrine ministry that manifests unambiguously the tradition of service articulated in both the words and life of Christ in the New Testament. The oldest and most venerable title of the pope, first adopted by Pope Gregory the Great, is *servus servorum Dei* – the servant of the servants of God.

It was stated in early 1996 by the Cardinal Secretary of State, Cardinal Sodano, that John Paul II 'had taken note' of requests from other religious leaders to find a 'new form' of exercising the Petrine ministry that would be open to 'a new situation'. Such a statement is unprecedented and heralds future developments which may surprise even the most optimistic supporters of Christian unity.

CATHOLICISM AND CONSCIENCE: ARE THEY COMPATIBLE?

In trying to answer the question 'Are Catholicism and conscience compatible?', I want to argue against two equally unacceptable extreme views: namely, a religious version of totalitarianism, on the one hand, and a widely prevalent and much-vaunted subjectivism on the other.

Among the many charges levelled at Catholicism, the one that most often renders it distasteful to many open-minded and intelligent individuals is the claim that Catholics aren't allowed to think for themselves. According to this charge, the Catholic conscience is caged, and freedom to hold views contrary to Catholic teaching is curtailed by an arbitrary authority vested in an inhibiting hierarchy. The Church, in other words, according to this view, is no better than a totalitarian regime, a less extreme version of Lenin's Bolshevik state.

In this claim, which must be taken seriously, the chief casualty is conscience and its rights. This is the value at the heart of post-Enlightenment, liberal democracy, that is trammelled, undermined and negated by Catholicism, it is alleged.

The second view against which I want to argue begins quite reasonably: it holds that the rights of conscience, both in belief and behaviour, are paramount. Nobody can insist that you believe anything you do not believe, and nobody can insist that you do anything or do not do anything, within the constraints of the law of course, that you want or do not want to do.

So far, so good; who in their right mind could disagree?

Indeed, we are fortunate enough to live in a state that so far at least guarantees these freedoms. But this view is often taken a step further. And the further step converts a sensible and sane view into an incoherent and contradictory one. This is when freedom of conscience shades into subjectivism: the view that whatever you believe to be true is, by that fact alone, true – for you; and whatever you think it is right and good to do is, by that fact alone, good – for you. The inevitable implication of this view is that there is no such thing as objective truth or anything that is objectively right or wrong. All is a matter of individual temperament, upbringing, predilection, propensity, preference and taste: and *de gustibus non est disputandum*.

Now in a quite understandable reaction against what has justifiably been perceived to be legalism and authoritarianism on the part of some elements of Catholic practice in the past, many Catholics have adopted a position over the understanding and practice of conscience that is, to all intents and purposes, subjectivist. They have come to understand the notion of conscience as a 'still small voice' within each of us, an inner oracle, beyond the reach of reason, indeed superior to reason, inviolable and infallible, and a sure guide to what is right and true – for me.

Now I want to say that both these extreme and opposed views are nonsense and dangerous. Let us start with the first view and let us be frank. Catholics in positions of authority and influence have sometimes been guilty, as have all kinds of other people outside Catholicism, of trying to stifle dissent, extirpate heresy by any means, including violence, and bludgeoning unbelief into submission by enforcing orthodoxy.

There have also been flawed and ineptly ambiguous attempts to express Catholic teaching that have served only to distort and obscure it, especially in the nineteenth century when modern political upheavals provoked genuine fear for the stability of society and the Church's place in the world. Pius IX's encyclical, *Quanta Cura* (1864), for instance, appears to be condemning liberty in all its forms whereas what he is really condemning is the anarchy so avidly preached and practised in the wake of then recent revolutions.

Now error should never be covered over or rationalized or excused, nor should evidence be reinterpreted to suit present exigencies. But neither should we ever wrench events or actions from their historical and psychological context. Nevertheless, despite the excesses of individuals in the past or the mindset of society in general, and not just that of the Church, at any given time, we need to be clear what the Catholic Church *actually* teaches on the matter of conscience.

And the fact is that no other religious body has declared as explicitly as the Catholic Church its belief in the sovereignty of conscience. The touchstone of orthodoxy on this point is the Second Vatican Council's *Declaration of Religious Freedom* (1965) which declares that nobody can be constrained to share a conviction that is not his or her own. This document's teaching is in line with Cardinal Newman's famous toast: 'to conscience first, and the pope afterwards'.

Of course, it is self-evident that you cannot believe what you do not believe. Assent to a belief can only be given freely, otherwise it is not assent and not a genuine belief. So much is logical. But in this document coercion by anybody or any institution, civil or religious, is expressly condemned and proscribed.

No less an authority than St Thomas Aquinas was crystal clear that though conscience can be mistaken, it always binds.[17] This means that one must always do what one considers to be *objectively* right. In other words, if I hold that a certain conviction is true I must live by it: to do otherwise would be to live a lie. St Thomas makes his point forcibly when he say that 'anyone upon whom the ecclesiastical authorities, in ignorance of the true facts, impose a demand that offends against his clear conscience, should perish in excommunication rather than violate his conscience'.

Equally, however, though conscience seeks what is *objectively* right, it does not guarantee that one has found it. Which brings us to the second unacceptable, extreme view: subjectivism in the guise of conscience. The essential feature of this view is that it decides what is right or true *for me*. Now it is true that each of us must take personal responsibility for our beliefs and behaviour. Nobody and nothing can take our place or replace our responsibility. But it certainly does not follow from this that there is no such thing as objective right and wrong, truth or falsity. Nor does it mean that I automatically know the difference simply by consulting my inner conscience, as if it were some unfailing oracle. On the contrary, I have to work hard to discover and understand what is true and what is good. I must seek to discover, in other words, what is objectively good – and do that;

what is objectively true – and believe that. And in doing this I must make allowance for being wrong sometimes. Hence the necessity of listening to whatever help and wisdom is available to me.

It is often said in defence of the subjectivist view of conscience which I have been criticizing that only this view is consistent with and guarantees those twin poles of liberal democracy, tolerance and freedom. Well, there is both a logical and a practical point to be made here. Tolerance can never be an end in itself: it cannot be an absolute. Tolerance and toleration have their natural and logical limits: otherwise, intolerance must be tolerated. And this is a self-contradiction.

Again, there is, practically speaking, no such thing as absolute freedom. No matter how sincerely I hold the conviction that human sacrifice and cannibalism are the pious duty of every right-minded person, the state, thank goodness, will not grant me freedom to engage in such practices. On the subjectivist's view, however, Adolf Hitler cannot be faulted for his anti-Semitic views: such views are neither true nor false. Nor can he really be faulted for the Final Solution: he was neither right nor wrong. The only question is whether he was sincere in his convictions or not.

Conscience binds, says St Thomas, but he also says that conscience is not always right. Conscience has often commanded the morally indefensible. Conscience has told many men to fight duels, to carry on blood feuds, to offer their children in human sacrifice or to persecute 'heretics' and to slaughter enemies. Manifestly, that something is a deliverance of conscience is no guarantee that it is right: there is much more to working out what is right.

This mythical notion of conscience is dangerous. Conscience is nothing more, and nothing less, than that act of judgement guided by reason and good sense, which may include reliance for good reasons on an authority, that something is objectively true and or right. Conscience, properly understood, is the demand we impose on ourselves for integrity. Through the exercise of conscience, we bring to bear on our decision-making an absolute perspective. It leads us beyond ourselves, opening us to reasoned consideration of questions pertaining to value and truth. It also leads us to take responsibility for our lives and actions. Conscience is the demand that we act on our best judgement.

But if conscience is not subjectivism neither is it scrupulosity. On the contrary, it directs us away from bigotry, unreasonableness and self-deception. But it does not in every case unfailingly issue in an accurate or right judgement, no more than our senses are always accurate. It requires training, education, experience and reflection. Conscience is sacred in the sense that each individual is sacred. We must strive to make the best judgement possible in all situations. And we must follow that judgement. God will do the rest.

THE ORDINATION OF WOMEN: WHY NOT?

From time to time, the Catholic Church adopts a position which would be a PR nightmare for even the most competent 'spin-doctor'. With steely disregard for political correctness, she expresses on occasion views diametrically opposed to the current of popular opinion. To some, both outside and within the Church, this constitutes unbridled arrogance. For others, it is consistent with the divinely mandated mission of the Church to preserve and hand on intact the *depositum fidei*, the Gospel of Jesus Christ. A conspicuous example of this concerns the ordination of women to the priesthood. As with many other questions, discussion of this topic is often marred by misinformation and distortion. Here I aim only to describe what the Church officially teaches on this subject and to offer some ideas about why it adopts this position.

In the apostolic letter, *Reserving Priestly Ordination to Men Alone,* John Paul II reaffirmed that the Church has no authority to confer priestly ordination on women. This teaching, it was said in the document, is to be held definitively by all the faithful as belonging to the deposit of faith. The Congregation for the Doctrine of the Faith later clarified the authority of this teaching by stating that it is founded on the authority of Scripture, has been constantly preserved and applied in the tradition of the Church, both East and West, Latin and Orthodox, and has been set forth infallibly by the ordinary magisterium.

Complaints are frequently heard that the Church is acting beyond its remit or power; that it too often overreaches itself, or is authoritarian in demanding more of people than is necessary. But this teaching is a declaration that it *cannot* do something, that it has not the *authority* to do something. In other words, the Church is here submitting itself to a higher authority: its Lord and his revelation.

Now the Catholic position on this question is neither recent nor unique to the Latin Church. On the contrary, it is a constant tradition and one that remains intact in both East and West, as far as both the Latin and Orthodox Churches are concerned. Where the ordination of women has been admitted and exercised it has been an independent initiative on the part of relatively recently formed bodies arising from the division of Christendom in Europe in the sixteenth century.

But what does it mean to say that a teaching 'belongs to the deposit of faith'? To say this is to affirm that it belongs to or is necessarily connected with what the Church has received from Christ. The Church believes that the sacraments – and holy orders or the priesthood is one of them – are entirely the gifts of Christ, not the result of ecclesiastical or human innovation. So the recently published *Catechism of the Catholic Church* (CCC 1117) says: 'As she has done for the canon of sacred Scripture and for the doctrine of the faith, the Church, by the power of the Spirit who guides her "into all truth", has gradually recognized this treasure [namely, the saving power of the sacraments] received from Christ and, as the faithful steward of God's mysteries, has determined its "dispensation".'

So the Church, over the centuries, has discerned seven sacraments, in the strict sense of the term, instituted by the Lord. In other words, the essentials of the celebration of these sacraments are matters which, like the canon of sacred Scripture and the doctrines of the faith, the Church has discerned and explained, but not invented or generated on her own authority. The Church calls these essential, constitutive elements the 'deposit' or treasury of the faith, which is Christ's legacy to his people and from which they continually draw life and sustenance. Scripture, sacraments and doctrines are gifts the Church has received and must guard.

At root, the reason why the Church can only ordain men to the priesthood is that she is bound to follow the example of Christ himself, who chose only men as apostles. Some light on this obligation can be shed if you think of another sacrament, the Eucharist. The all-important aspect of this sacrament is that this is what Christ himself did, using these elements, bread and wine, and these words, the words of institution. The Church does not imagine herself having invented or devised this: the liturgy surrounding it, yes, but not the heart of the Eucharist enshrined in the many different liturgical forms.

This raises a more fundamental point: the Church's existence is rooted in actual historical events, played out in contingent, historical circumstances, and rooted in time. Christ is an actual human being; this is the whole point of the Incarnation. His death is recalled as having taken place at a particular moment in history, in definite, specifiable circumstances; hence the mention in the Creed of an otherwise insignificant and long-forgotten, minor Roman provincial official, Pontius Pilate. The Church therefore cannot escape certain facts: she cannot reinvent herself or the heart of her belief. This is received. The Church cannot determine the recipients of priestly ordination in a manner that contradicts the actions of Christ himself, its originator.

But, it may be asked, was not this choice of Christ wholly determined by the cultural circumstances of the time? What is distinctive and most evident about Christ in the Gospels is that he often demonstrated his freedom from the cultural and religious conventions of his time. And even when he chose publicly to observe them, it was by way of bringing them to fulfilment or in order to reveal the true but concealed point and purpose of them, not to accommodate himself to them. His teaching on the sabbath and sexual morality are good examples of this independence from prevailing cultural mores. There seems no good reason, therefore, to suggest that the choice of men as apostles was a cultural accommodation. As early as the second century the topic of female ordination was raised and openly debated and these discussions were part of what led to the constant practice of the Church, recently reaffirmed by the pope.

Perhaps the loudest clamour against this teaching of the Catholic Church is that it offends against justice at a time when we are more sensitive than ever to the social oppression of women. But is there an injustice involved in limiting ordination to men? Justice is the moral virtue that accords what is due to both God and neighbour. Justice and giving what is due are often understood exclusively in terms of equality – equal rights, equal pay, equal protection under the law. And this follows from the conviction that every person has equal dignity, from which certain rights flow. This equality of dignity is also a facet of the

Church's life: all the baptized are equal in dignity, equally called to communion with God, and equally called to holiness and fullness of life in God.

The question of justice in connection with the Church's teaching that it cannot ordain women arises only if you think that all or any human being or all or any of the baptized have a *right* to be ordained. Clearly, there is no civic right to be ordained on the part of any citizen. But nor is there a right rooted in any aspect of the Church's nature or the shared vocation of all Christians. Not being ordained does not in any way contradict the call to holiness or constitute an obstacle to fullness of life and communion with God. An old-fashioned but still useful way of expressing this is to say that ordination is not necessary for salvation. To deprive someone of what is necessary for salvation most certainly would be a grave injustice.

Frequently, the priesthood in this discussion is considered under the heading of 'leadership' and 'power', and the exclusion of women from ordination thus constitutes their exclusion from leadership roles and influence in the Church. But this description of the priesthood comes perilously close to assimilating it to the leadership roles legitimately and appropriately played in the secular world. And this is to distort fatally the nature of the priesthood.

Now in the Gospels our Lord offers to every baptized person a radical and revolutionary way of understanding ourselves and our relationships. Far from lording it over one another, we are to be, like him, servants, feet-washers, ministers to one another. The word he uses is *diakonos*: waiter at table, doing that which is needed, not that which merits praise or reward and much less a flattering obituary. We are to be servants of one another not in the sense of 'servants of the Crown' or 'public servants' to which status and admiration and dignity are accorded, but menial servants, doing that which is needed without calculation and without safeguards to our dignity. This is to render the service Christ has rendered us; this is the priesthood of all believers, by which all the baptized participate in the life of Christ, which has been poured out for us. And, within the priesthood of all believers, there is another kind of specific service, which is a continuation of that service rendered by the apostles chosen by Christ himself. But this service does not have status in any worldly sense and it is both a mistake to think it does and a deformation of the role to seek it for that reason.

A clue to what the priesthood is lies in the fact that, until recently, clerics received the tonsure as a mark of their clerical state. The tonsure was worn by Roman slaves, to prevent them from escaping and to mark them out as someone's property. When he became a bishop, St Augustine said openly: 'With you I am a Christian and this is for me a consolation; for you I am a bishop and this is for me a danger.'

The inability of the Church to ordain women to the priesthood must not, however, be allowed to inhibit the search for new and constructive ways in which the contribution of women to the Church's life, mission and ministry can be made. Teaching, diplomacy, canon law and formation are all vital areas of the Church's life where the absence of women can only be considered an impoverishment.

ANNULMENT: DIVORCE BY ANOTHER NAME?

Fewer people are marrying. In England and Wales there were fewer first marriages in 1992 than in 1892, even though the population grew by three quarters during that century. In ten years' time, if current trends continue, married people will be in the minority of the population for the first time since records began. At the same time, cohabitation has risen. It is estimated that currently over a million and a half people are cohabiting; by 2021 that is expected to rise to about three million people.

At the same time, during this same period, divorces have risen exponentially. There were 25,000 divorces annually in England and Wales in 1961; in 1995 there were 155,000. There is now one divorce for every two marriages and Britain has the highest divorce rate in the European Union. These same trends are widespread throughout Europe yet there is still no consensus as to why.

These statistics must provoke unease. But the discussion of this situation rarely raises the most important question: namely, what is marriage, anyway? Failure to come to grips with this question is also at the root of much misunderstanding about the Catholic Church's practice of granting nullities through its tribunals by which a marriage is declared to have been invalid from the beginning. Effectively, it is a declaration that there was never a marriage in the first place. It should be said that this misunderstanding is shared by many Catholics themselves.

It is alleged that the Catholic Church is being disingenuous and dishonest by claiming, on the one hand, that marriage is indissoluble while, on the other hand, offering to some people the possibility of second marriage via the nullity procedure. This charge often arises from confusion about the nature of marriage and the role of the law, both civil and canonical, in articulating and protecting the reality of marriage.

The evolution of our understanding of marriage and the law surrounding it is a complex topic which brings together theological, legal, social and historical elements. Even as late as the twelfth century theologians were still discussing and disagreeing about what constituted a marriage: is it consent or consummation or both? And still, Western Christianity differs from Eastern Christianity in asserting that what makes the marriage is the exchange of consent of the two people, while the East says it is constituted by the conferral of the sacrament by the priest.

Again, even in the Catholic Church, the presence of a priest and the performance of the marriage rite was unnecessary for validity before the Council of Trent in 1563. And only in 1754, after the Hardwicke Marriage Act had been passed, was a ceremony a legal requirement in England and Wales.

What does the Catholic Church teach about the nature of marriage? *The Catechism of the Catholic Church* echoes the *Code of Canon Law* when it says that marriage is

> **a covenant by which a man and a woman establish between themselves a partnership of the whole of life, by its very nature ordered toward the good of the spouses and the procreation and education of offspring; this covenant between baptised persons has been raised by Christ to the dignity of a sacrament.**
>
> *(Catechism* 1601*; Code* 1055.1*)*

And the first property of this covenant emphasized by the Church is its indissolubility:

> **Thus the marriage bond has been established by God himself in such a way that a marriage concluded and consummated between baptised persons can never be dissolved. This bond, which results from the free human act of the spouses and their consummation of the marriage, is a reality, henceforth**

irrevocable and gives rise to a covenant guaranteed by God's fidelity. The Church does not have the power to contravene this disposition of divine wisdom.

(Catechism 1640*)*

Another statement of the Church's teaching on the nature of marriage is in the controversial encyclical, *Humanae Vitae.* There it is stated that marriage is *fully human,* arising from a unity of heart and soul seeking together to attain their human fulfilment; *total,* sharing everything with a love that excludes selfishness and unreasonable exception; *faithful and exclusive* until death; and creative of life, intending to bring new life into being.

Now the law of the Church, its Canon Law, translates this human reality into juridical terms. And, briefly, it states that in order to enter validly into this marriage covenant, the parties concerned must be free from any impediment (Cann. 1083-1094); must exchange proper consent (Cann. 1095-1103); and must, if one or both of them are Catholic, do so according to canonical form (Cann. 1108-1127). The absence of any of these essential requirements renders the marriage null and invalid.

The work of the marriage tribunal in a diocese is, when petitioned, to investigate whether or not there are grounds for declaring a marriage null for these reasons. Nullity procedures are appropriately extensive and thorough because it is required that actual proof or at least moral certainty is obtained. The presumption, in other words, is always in favour of the validity of the marriage in question.

So what are the possible grounds for nullity? Given the nature of marriage, there are obviously certain impediments to contracting a marriage. Some of these apply to everybody because they affect the natural reality of marriage; others apply only to Catholics because they affect the sacramental reality of marriage. About the former the Church cannot do anything; but from the latter kind of impediments she can, in certain specified situations, dispense. The two in the former category, that is, in the order of the natural reality of marriage, are first, the existence of a previous bond of marriage and, secondly, impotence. Impotence is an impediment, however, only if it is antecedent and perpetual. Sterility, however, does not affect validity.

All other impediments, with the exception of some concerning consanguinity and affinity, are of an ecclesiastical nature and so bind only Catholics and those wishing to marry a Catholic, and can be dispensed. So, for instance, though the civil requirements are observed generally, according to Canon Law you have to be a minimum age to marry validly (sixteen and fourteen for males and females respectively); there has to be a dispensation when a Catholic marries an unbaptized person; and an attempted marriage that involves a priest vowed to celibacy, or anybody solemnly vowed to celibacy, is invalid. And you need a dispensation if you want to marry your first cousin. So the Church could declare a marriage null if it was entered into invalidly on account of the presence of any of these impediments without dispensation.

The more usual grounds for nullity, however, are based on the absence of positive conditions necessary for validity. The crucial conditions concern consent: the exchange of consent must be free, and the parties must have the capacity, the knowledge and the will to exchange such a consent. If there is a defect in any of these conditions, the marriage is null. The law also refers to an increasingly common ground for nullity: it speaks of 'a grave lack of discretion of judgement concerning the rights and obligations of marriage which are to be mutually given and accepted.' (Cann. 1095.2)

So, for instance, if someone entered marriage because of pressure due to pregnancy, or in order to escape the parental home or on the rebound from a previous relationship or under the influence of alcohol or drugs or if he or she was too young and immature to make a lifelong commitment, the tribunal may find sufficient evidence to prove that such a person was gravely lacking in the judgement required to enter marriage. Sometimes, the grounds will be of a strictly psychological nature which impede the free exchange of consent.

A marriage would be invalid if one of the parties deceived the other into thinking something to be the case about them which was untrue. This, of course, would have to be a grave matter and one about which one of the parties could honestly say: 'If I'd known that I'd never have married him or her.' Again, if you married the wrong person by mistake – someone's twin sister, for instance – it would be invalid. Again, a marriage would be invalid if it were entered into simply to obtain a visa or social security benefits. But also, a marriage would be invalid if someone did not commit themselves exclusively to this one person:

if, for instance, they intended to continue in another relationship incompatible with the marriage. It would invalidate a marriage if one of the parties intended to be unfaithful, or harboured at the time of the marriage the formed intention to seek a divorce if the marriage did not work out. A marriage would also be invalid if one or other of the parties firmly intended, permanently and for the whole of the marriage, to exclude the possibility of children. Lastly and most obviously a marriage is invalid if it is entered into due to force or grave fear. In all these cases, the consent would be defective and the marriage would therefore be invalid and it would be for the marriage tribunal to prove, if asked to do so by one of the partners, that one or all of these conditions obtained at the time of the marriage.

So, far from being divorce by another name, marriage annulment in the Catholic Church rests on its conviction that marriage has a definite and specific nature, and that it is a serious business, requiring certain essential conditions and dispositions. Far from detracting from the grave nature of marriage, the marriage tribunals exist because marriage is too important to be taken for granted and entered into lightly.

CHRISTIANITY AND WORLD RELIGIONS: CAN THEY ALL BE TRUE?

Pluralism is a commonplace of our lives and a cherished value of our age: something to be celebrated, encouraged and desired, a mark of modern man's maturity and a welcome departure from his former xenophobia and the many violent reactions this has prompted in our history.

But, for many, pluralism has lent plausibility to the central tenet of what has become known as 'post-modernism': namely, the view that there is no such thing as objective truth: only your truth and my truth, our truth and their truth. This epistemological position combines in differing measures elements of both relativism and subjectivism but the upshot of this position is that the world is made up only of contingencies, relativities, and intepretation. We have no access to anything outside our own culture and language. And so this facet of modern life in which more and more ethnic and religious variety is the chief characteristic of all Western societies has seemed to many to carry with it an undermining of foundational values in which 'everything is contingent, a product of history and open to reassessment'[18] and the truth is human, socially produced, historically developed, plural and changing. The notion of an ultimate truth is incompatible with the fluid and transient nature of language and 'the world is an argument that never gets settled'.[19]

For those who espouse this view, the two areas of life in which they see their position most explicitly realized are ethics and religion. There is, in both, an infinite variety of standpoints and opinions, none having any more validity or truth than the other. One religion is as good or bad as another: they are all as true or false as one another.

This is the pressing background against which a very important aspect of Christian theology and understanding has been developing in our own day. How does Christianity view other religions? Is Christianity one religion among others? What kind of understanding is available to us that avoids both relativism on the one hand and imperialism on the other?

In one sense this is far from being a new problem. The Christian Gospel was first preached in a world awash with religious movements. The Hellenistic era was an age of anxiety, like our own, in which traditional securities, both social and religious, were being rapidly eroded. The state religions were giving way to more comforting religious phenomena which met the need for reassurance. In this setting, there was keen competition among rival religions and philosophies, all offering the secret of the good life. Christianity was seen, especially by the rather sniffy, cultured and traditionalist figures of the time, as a low-grade, populist movement just like all the others that were springing up around the Roman world. But as soon as Christianity began to break away from its Jewish roots and encounter the wider Hellenistic world, it had to come to grips with this question of how to understand itself in relation to the great religious tradition that is Judaism.

We are faced with a similar task. In the English-speaking world especially, we have been cosseted by a certain parochialism throughout the nineteenth and early twentieth centuries. Now, through immigration from former colonies, Great Britain is home to increasing numbers of adherents to the great world religions. The resulting multiculturalism once again demands fresh understanding. So what, in practice and in principle, is the attitude of the Catholic Church to other religions?

The Catholic Church is unique in making an official and binding statement on the matter. The Second Vatican Council included in its teaching a whole document devoted to this: *Nostra Aetate* (1965), though it does not develop the theme in detail, nevertheless lays down the principles that should guide our understanding in this area.

The crucial starting-points that set the perspective are the following all-encompassing facts. First, all people, without exception, have a single origin and goal, namely, God. Secondly, God wills that all should receive his salvation. So, *Nostra Aetate* (1) says:

> **All nations are one community and have one origin, because God caused the whole human race to dwell on the whole face of the earth. They also have one final end, God, whose providence, manifestation of goodness and plans for salvation are extended to all, until the elect be gathered together in the holy city which the bright light of God will illuminate and where the people will walk in his light.**
>
> (Tanner vol. 2, p.968)

It cannot be that God should will this and yet not afford the means to this salvation. So is it the case that all religions, without exception, are means to salvation? First, recent scholarship, not necessarily Catholic scholarship, has concluded that the term 'religion' is problematic. Nobody has yet formulated a universally applicable and satisfactory definition of what constitutes a religion. At least, nobody has so far come up with a definition that can encompass all those traditions we usually call religions. So one difficulty with that question is the equally difficult question to which it gives rise: to what are we referring when we ask it? It is not easy to know.

Nevertheless, leaving this aside, *Nostra Aetate* (2) unambiguously says:

> **The Catholic Church rejects nothing of those things which are true and holy in these religions. It regards with respect those ways of acting and living and those precepts and teachings which, though often at variance with what it holds and expounds,**

> **frequently reflect a ray of truth which enlightens everyone. Yet, without ceasing, it preaches, and is bound to preach, Christ who is "the way, the truth and the life" (Jn 14:6), in whom people find the fullness of religious life and in whom God has reconciled all things to himself.**
>
> (Tanner vol.2, p.969)

In other words, the Church acknowledges the presence of God and his grace and providence throughout his creation. But the source of that grace is always Christ, the Incarnate Word of God. The Church cannot believe otherwise if it also believes that Christ is God. Religious movements, when genuinely motivated, can be seen as human responses to the all-encompassing and universal presence and action of God throughout his creation, of which he is the sole ground and ultimate meaning and fulfilment. But the Church believes that the Incarnation of God among us is God's doing and it is precisely because of the Incarnation that we can recognize the presence and providence of a loving God within his creation.

And this is precisely what is unique about Christianity. Only Christ, as the Word of God made human, accounts for the fact that God, who is totally other and transcends his creation, can also be experienced from within this world; consciously by mystics, unconsciously by graced individuals, without persons losing their identity and becoming subsumed into God.[20] The Incarnation is the archetype of a new form of relationship between God and the human being.

> **Here lies the scandal of particularity: while the mystical practices of the other world religions are designed to facilitate the laying aside of material impedimenta so as to let being be reabsorbed into the world's origin, Christianity alone dares to contradict this programme by its assertion of a God who entered into and became a part of history, making his own body, on the Cross, the unique bridge between the finite and infinite realms... Only in Christ, in whom all apparent opposites are unified without mingling, can the partial insights of the various world religions reach a satisfactory account of the God-world relation.[21]**

PART II
The Ten Commandments

HUMAN FLOURISHING

It is no longer fashionable to approach the question of the Catholic Church's moral teaching by way of the Ten Commandments. For one thing, such an approach might tend to confirm the widespread view that, for Catholics, morality is concerned exclusively with being told imperiously what you should not do. You could be forgiven for thinking that the Ten Commandments epitomize this 'don't do that' approach, with their repeated 'Thou shalt nots'. The negative impression is compounded by the caricature of Catholic morality which depicts it as concerned especially with what you should not do in the area of sex. Catholics have only themselves to blame for this widespread mis-impression, given the less than satisfactory way the Catholic moral tradition has often been presented.

But the Ten Commandments, far from being mere prohibitions imposed by a curmudgeonly, pleasure-hating God and his ecclesiastical agents, are actually foundational principles for civilized existence: that is, for human flourishing according to the kind of nature we all share. And so, unfashionable as it may be, I want to use the Ten Commandments as a background for talking about basic issues of morality and, in the process, I want to show that the Catholic moral tradition is richer, more humane, more open and more intellectually rigorous than its bad press usually suggests.

Without wanting to labour the point, let me take an example of the negative perspective and show how unfaithful it is to the Catholic moral tradition. One particular distortion is the view that, at root, morality concerns laws, duties and obligations to be observed, fulfilled and satisfied. These requirements, it is thought, are imposed arbitrarily by a God whose chief role is law enforcement and the meting out of justice in the negative form of punishment now and, most dreadfully, for all eternity. This is a

God towards whom the only sensible attitude to adopt is fear and obedience. The kind of human being that emerges from life-long adherence to such a regime is, inevitably, infantile and anxious.

Now, however much this may have characterized the views of some individuals, it could never be thought of as a Catholic view: indeed, it was not even present in the Old Testament view of morality. Nevertheless, it is a view into which it is all too easy to fall if certain key principles in our understanding are skewed.

The Jews, for instance, never thought that punishment for sin came from a punishing God. Rather, they understood whatever of a negative kind happened as a consequence of sin to be an extension or after-effect of the sinful action itself. In just the same way, they viewed reward as something that resulted from good deeds themselves. If they prospered, it was a natural effect of good choices and right conduct.

Again, their moral code, exemplified in the Ten Commandments, was regarded not as an imposition but as a gift that was of benefit to them and intended by God as such. The Law, in other words, was given not for God's benefit, but for theirs. The Ten Commandments were not some divine whim by which God would judge who was in and who out but pointers to the conditions that make for a peaceful and flourishing existence in harmony with all around you. Though they were given by God, they are rational conclusions at which one could arrive simply by the exercise of reason and wisdom and reflection on experience. In this sense, they sum up the most basic demands of our nature as social animals and they establish the most basic perspective within which to understand ourselves.

What is particularly interesting is that they point to relationships as the natural goal of human existence: our relationship with God and the network of relationships of all kinds among ourselves. So the first three commandments establish the contours of our relationship with the Creator and the other seven establish the outlines for all our other relationships.

What is also significant is the context of the Ten Commandments. Remember, in the biblical narrative, they are given just after the Israelites have been finally liberated from slavery in Egypt. Now for the Jews the Exodus is the fulcrum around which the whole understanding of man's relationship with God revolves, both in real, historical terms and in symbolical terms. This is the decisive, saving act that binds the people to God, setting them apart as his Chosen People. They enter into a covenant with him and the Ten Commandments are given to them as a charter for freedom, deliverance, and for flourishing in their new liberated state. By the Exodus, God shows himself to be not just their Creator but their Redeemer, who demonstrates his love by delivering them from slavery: and the Ten Commandments are part of his gift of deliverance.

Now I have said a lot about an Old Testament view of these things. But this same view persists in Christianity, and is actually taken even further along the same path. Remember the incident in the Gospels when the religious leaders try to trap our Lord by getting him to answer a trick question so that they would have grounds on which to condemn him. 'Teacher,' they ask him, 'which commandment in the law is the greatest?' He answers, 'You shall love the Lord your God with all your heart, and with all your soul, and with all your mind. This is the greatest and first commandment. And the second is like it: You shall love your neighbour as yourself. On these two commandments hang all the law and the prophets' (Matt. 22:35-40).

There could be no more explicit and unequivocal statement of the foundation of Christian morality. Whatever else is said, the ultimate test of its authority and authenticity must surely be whether or not it is consistent with this statement by our Lord himself. That this was from the earliest times understood to be the litmus test is obvious in something St Paul says: 'Owe no one anything except to love one another: for the one who loves another has fulfilled the law. The commandments "You shall not commit adultery; You shall not murder; You shall not steal; You shall not covet": and any other commandment, are summed up in this word, "Love your neighbour as yourself." Love does no wrong to a neighbour; therefore, love is the fulfilling of the law' (Rom. 13:8-10).

Again, that this was taken seriously is clear from the understanding such an important and influential figure as St Thomas Aquinas had of the Catholic moral tradition. The first question with which morality is concerned, according to Aquinas is not, What is my duty? What are my obligations? But, In what does happiness consist for human beings, built as we are with minds that seek to understand, hearts that long to love and be loved, and bodies that express all of this outwardly? Morality for

Aquinas, in other words, is rooted in the most basic and universal desire shared by every human being: the desire for happiness and fulfilment. So we need to know what is genuinely fulfilling of our human nature and how this is to be achieved. And this is the business of ethical reflection.

Aquinas's pursuit of these questions gives rise to an ethic, not of duty, but of opportunity: opportunity, that is, for human flourishing, an ethic rooted in our human nature rather than in an externally imposed law. This establishes a distinctive perspective within which human needs and experience at all levels are taken seriously. The very stuff of morality, its raw material, is the human nature with which we have been endowed by God: and the point and purpose of moral reflection is to discern ways in which this nature can flourish.

For Aquinas, the pinnacle of the moral life is the life of friendship: friendship with God and with each other. And he means that word in all its richness. He regards friendship as the fullness and fulfilment of love, the perfect communion of persons. Only this gives us perfect happiness.

Now this is the antidote to some of the distortions that have so often passed as a Catholic view of morality. Within this view, Aquinas can say, for instance, that God is not offended by anything we do, except those things that harm us. In other words, his view is that of a solicitous father, not a stern judge. He says that virtue is its own reward: we seek to flourish because we want to be happy and fulfilled, not just because we want to please or, worse, appease God. And like any solicitous friend, God desires our happiness as an end in itself.

GOD: NOT IDOLS, MAGIC OR PERFORMANCE

The Ten Commandments define us in terms of our relationships. The first three commandments – I am the Lord your God. You shall have no other gods before me. You shall not take the name of the Lord your God in vain. Remember the sabbath and keep it holy – all concern our relationship with God.

This is an obvious and straightforward first step, you might think. Not so. Not so because of this tricky word 'God'. That there is more to it than meets the eye is clear from the word used in the deliverance of these commandments to Moses. When Moses asks God his name, he is given the gnomic reply, 'I AM WHO I AM' and he instructs Moses to say 'I AM has sent me to you'. Now this may seem like pseudo-metaphysical sophistry. But in fact it is a periphrasis for the One who is un-nameable. Indeed, in some Hebrew texts of the Bible, you will see gaps where the word 'God' should be and some ultra-Orthodox Jews will not utter the divine name at all.

This same hesitancy and reticence continues in Christianity; or it should, if we are being faithful to both tradition and reason. Sadly, as we have seen, it is for many a forgotten perspective. The one word around which there is the greatest intellectual problematic is the one word most glibly used by both protagonists of religious belief and it opponents. This carelessness about the word and its appropriate use has two serious results: it renders much theological talk implausible and unintelligible – theology becomes theological science fiction – and it makes atheism a perfectly reasonable option. By which I mean that many who reject belief in God as untenable reject a caricature and nonsense, as they should. What they reject is the notion that there is, as the Dominican, Herbert McCabe once famously wrote, a Top Person in the universe, a celestial Louis XIV or a Grand Architect, like Basil Spence only bigger and more powerful. As McCabe said then, 'If denying this claim makes you an atheist, then I and Thomas Aquinas and a whole Christian tradition are atheists too'.[22]

Let me elaborate. From the beginning, at the burning bush, to the present, it has always been understood in the Judaeo-Christian tradition that the word 'God' is the most difficult of words to use well, that is, with both sense and integrity.[23] Why? Because the finite nature of our minds and the inadequacy of our language mean that we are always at risk of anthropomorphism. The word 'God' refers to that ineffable mystery which grounds and embraces the whole of existence, including our own. Now theologians in particular are often accused of invoking 'mystery' when they lack a suitable and satisfying explanation. By 'mystery' I don't mean just a temporary gap in our knowledge and understanding. I mean, rather, that which lies permanently beyond all our understanding and language – that which is, in principle and not just in practice, for the moment, imponderable and impenetrable – and yet permanently present because presupposed to everything else. It refers to the abiding question that remains when all individual questions have been answered, the goal beyond all individual goals we reach for, the goodness beyond all the individual good things of life and the truth in which all individual truths have their home and to which they tend. And the promise that selfless love will be neither defeated nor frustrated nor disappointed.

These first three commandments, therefore, establish that God is the ultimate ground of reality and, as such, uniquely worthy of worship and love. They thus set the broadest possible context and perspective within which life is to be understood and lived and they establish the most important, the most basic and all-encompassing of all our relationships: namely, that between Creator and creature.

But they do even more than this. Irreducibly basic as the relationship between Creator and creature is, it still leaves an ineluctable question unanswered. Reason can lead us to the conviction that our existence is not self-sufficient, not self-explanatory. We can arrive at the reasonable conclusion that our existence is dependent and derivative, that there must be a One on whom our existence depends at every moment.

But having arrived at this conclusion, we may still entertain the possibility that this One on whom everything and everyone depends for existence is, like Aristotle's god, uncaring, unfeeling, cold, distant and removed from what he has created. Indeed, given the presence of evil in the world and in ourselves, it might seem there are very good grounds for thinking in this way. But what this first commandment establishes is that this Creator's act of creation, both at the beginning and even now, is a work of love. In the Israelite context he proves his love by liberating them from slavery in Egypt. In the Christian context his love is proven by the selfless love and self-sacrifice of his Son. In other words, the abiding mystery that embraces our lives is not a dark empty abyss or the threatening absence of light, but the profoundly mysterious depth of selfless love.

Given this, the reason for the admonition concerning idols is obvious. Nobody worships an idol purposely: you worship what you think is or what you want to be 'God'. The warning against idols, therefore, alerts us to the danger of mistaking something for God: an idea, a formula, another person, an institution, a dogma, a dream, a project or a particular aspect of our lives or whatever. It directs us to God himself, and invites us to set our hearts on him.[24] Manifestly, given the meaning of the word 'God', lasting happiness and fulfilment is to be found only in him.

What about the admonition not to take the Lord's name in vain? This does not concern foul language and robust Anglo-Saxon expressions: it does not even concern, primarily, blasphemy. What it concerns first and foremost is telling the truth. Jews used the name of God, as we do still, in the taking of oaths. To invoke God's name in the telling of a lie is to dethrone God and make an idol of our own purposes. Similarly, to invoke God's name as a charm or spell or curse is to dethrone God and make him an element within a more fundamental system or scheme.

Again, the admonition to keep the sabbath holy concerns not activity as such, as it came to be in the rabbinical schools, but to avoid work – 'trade' is the word used. In other words, it is a warning against another form of idolatry. Do not worship the god of performance, efficiency, achievement and success. And do not fall prey to the temptation to judge yourself and others by this most superficial and misleading criterion. How apposite that is in the competitive meritocracy in which we find ourselves in the modern world. Remember St Paul's saying: 'By the grace of God I am what I am'. And St Francis's saying that a man is what he is before God, nothing more and nothing less.

PARENTS: HONOUR THEM, DESPITE PHILIP LARKIN

The first three commandments concern the most fundamental relationship in which we exist, namely, our relationship with God, outside of which nothing has meaning or sense. The remaining seven concern all our other relationships which are located by the commandments within the context of our relationship with God. The first of these remaining seven, the fourth commandment, alerts us to the most fundamental relationship *within* creation itself: namely, that of offspring to parents. Of all the commandments this is the most terse: honour your father and mother.

Now some have rather cynically seen here an injunction that merely endorses conventional social arrangements and legitimizes the basic authority figures of a patriarchal society. But it is clear from the placing of this commandment that a great deal hangs on it, so we need to ask ourselves what this particular commandment is getting at, and which values it is preserving. In what sense is our relationship with our parents fundamental and what does it mean, precisely, to honour them?

Clearly it is not intended that we think of our relationship with our parents as fundamental in the simplistic sense of taking precedence over all other relationships. We know that this cannot be the case, in principle, because it is explicitly said that a man leaves his father and mother and becomes one flesh with his wife. And in our own turn, some of us become parents ourselves. No, the relationship with our parents is fundamental in the sense that it is fixed and unchangeable: our parents are for ever our parents, and we are for ever their children. Nothing can change this. Remember how, in Russian, you are always referred to as the son of your father.

But, secondly, we are being exhorted never to forget that our lives are not of our own making: we are begotten, not manufactured, and we can never be exclusively the product of our own fashioning. Life, in other words, is a gift, not a possession. We are dependent, not in the sense of infantile need, but in the sense of being part of a larger whole.

Now acknowledging this relationship with our parents, and honouring them, is determinative of a whole perspective within which we see our lives. It shields us from the illusion of self-sufficiency and the kind of rank individualism that contributes so powerfully to that sense of homelessness and isolation so common in prosperous industrialized Western societies. To see ourselves as generated from our forbears is to register that we owe a great deal to others and have a responsibility to make our own contribution for future generations. Due acknowledgement of our debts to our parents and appropriate honour accorded to them reminds us of that healthy inter-dependence which we deny at our peril. So just as observing the sabbath was a way of remembering that time is a gift, so this injunction forcefully reminds us that the self-made man or woman is a lie. In those things that matter most we are always standing on the shoulders of others.

Erasmus says somewhere that after God the highest honour is to be paid to our parents. That we are dependent on our parents for the life we now experience is a powerful reminder of our dependence on God. And it is the folly of denying this or seeking to escape it that constitutes the original sin in the Garden of Eden.

The problem is that dependence is a dirty word for many of us. It clashes with the most cherished ideal of modern self-understanding, the free, unattached, sovereign, choosing individual. Dependency is confused with infantilism and is thought to be detrimental to our development as mature individuals. Well, of course, slavish dependence *is* to be avoided, but *inter*-dependence is a fact of life. And with it comes mutual and reciprocal responsibility. At birth we human beings, among all other animals, are the most dependent and the least adept at feeding and caring for ourselves for the longest time. This phase passes (for most of us) and we ourselves then assume the same responsibilities of care and nurture. But we can never set aside or repay the debts we incur at this level and to honour our parents is to acknowledge these debts.

Now a lot of what I am saying may seem to fit uneasily with that topic dear to psychology, the dysfunctional family. But one often feels that such talk is premised on the supposition that there is such a thing as the perfect or even just normal family. I think Carl Jung's remark about the normal man applies equally to the family: show me a normal man, he said, and I'll cure him.

Families, like human individuals, are imperfect. To uphold so-called 'family values' is not to deny this but it is to recognize the vital importance, for good or for ill, of the family situation in which we find ourselves. Being a parent is perhaps the most difficult and taxing role anybody ever plays in life. It demands that you give all you have to give without cramping the growth of your offspring as unique individuals, distinct and often very different from you. This takes both sensitivity and strength of character.

On the subject of overbearing parents, there is a story told of a famous rabbi whose father was a humble tailor. At a meeting of rabbis each quoted something from Torah learning, prefacing his remarks with: 'My saintly father said.' When his turn came, the rabbi wryly declared: 'My saintly father said, it is better for a boy to have a suit tailored specially for him than to give him his father's hand-me-downs.' No parent ever gets it right, but this does not vitiate the injunction to honour our parents.

Of course, our relationship with our parents goes through

many different stages until it eventually leads to a complete reversal of roles. But a vital step in our relationship with them is when we finally come to see them as equals: equals, that is, as human beings. An adult relationship with our parents involves our seeing them as human beings like ourselves, with weaknesses and failings, gifts and strengths. We must come to have a sense of solidarity rooted in the recognition that they have endured the burdens we have to carry. The reversal of roles comes about when we begin to look after them and they become dependent on us, as we once were on them. By this time, of course, we usually have children of our own and thus the primeval circle of generation is complete.

One final point: this commandment enjoins equal honour for mothers and fathers. This is an unusual feature in the wider society of the Middle East, where women were primarily instruments of male procreation and expendable slaves. The tone is set here, therefore, for a significantly different kind of relationship between husband and wife as well as between parents and children.

VALUE HUMAN LIFE – ALL OF IT

After the first three commandments, the other seven lay down the minimum requirements for social existence. The injunction to honour our parents emphasized that our lives are gifts, not something of our own making. But that gift, once having been received, must be reverenced and understood aright. So it is that this next commandment, though expressed negatively and minimally – Thou shalt not kill – affirms the intrinsic value of human life.

Now one problem with the way Catholic ethical teaching is presented is that it often starts with what we are *against* instead of starting with what we are *for* and what we *value*. There is much to learn here from Jewish life: most people would readily characterize Judaism by certain values, like the family and solidarity, rather than prohibitions. So, in this case, we oppose death-dealing activities because we are in awe of the gift and promise of life and such practices undermine everything we hope for.

In the past, killing was thought of as offensive because it violated the prerogative and right of God. Now, we see that this states only part of the case against killing innocent life. The fact is that human life is sacred in its own right precisely because it involves a relationship with God. To be at all is to be in this relationship. We value life because we value, in ourselves and in others, a relationship with God. To kill is to interfere with that relationship, to come between a person and God. And this is far from being of significance only for the individual. The inalienable right to life of every innocent person is the foundation of any civil society: to deny this right therefore jeopardizes the concept of law itself and the order needed for social survival.

Perhaps of all the commandments this one stands in the starkest contrast to the way of the world around us. This is surely the most violent culture ever created. More people have been killed by their own governments in this century than in any war. And this includes the unborn. Analysts and commentators of all faiths and none register among the ills of modernity the widespread breakdown of personal communication, the emergence of increasing and uncontrollable violence, the spreading phenomenon of depression and the rise of suicide among the young, and most recently, the return of genocide as the final solution to racial and tribal disputes. The conspiracy against life has, if anything, broadened and deepened.

But within supposedly civilized states, precisely when the inviolable rights of the person are solemnly proclaimed and the value of life is publicly affirmed, the very right to life is being denied or trampled upon, especially at the most significant moments of existence: the moment of birth and the moment of death. In his encyclical *Evangelium Vitae,* the pope contrasts the culture of life and the culture of death and he points to the exaggerated claims for choice and individual freedom as the root causes of the culture of death's flourishing.

In another encyclical, *Veritatis Splendor,* the pope locates the problem in the severing of any link between objective truth and freedom understood in the context of democracy exclusively in terms of the rule of the majority. The upshot of this severance is moral relativism. Thus the significance and importance of seeking what is objectively true is contested, and freedom alone, uprooted from any objectivity, is left to decide for itself what is good and what is evil (*Veritatis Splendor* 84*).* This necessarily renders those who cannot exercise freedom of choice vulnerable – hence abortion and euthanasia are the crucial symptoms.

These are not new, of course, but the call for legal recognition is. They are now regarded as 'legitimate expressions of human freedom, to be acknowledged and protected as actual rights' (*Evangelium Vitae* 18). Decriminalization of abortion, for instance, has now led to abortion being enshrined in legal systems as a legal right, practically without qualification: a position even the framers of the original legislation never envisaged. A crime against life thus becomes a right of individual freedom. So democracy edges towards totalitarianism because the will of the majority is now imposed on the minority and, as a consequence, the safeguard of just relations among people is destroyed. 'A democracy without values easily turns into open or thinly disguised totalitarianism' (*Veritatis Splendor* 101). Respect for individual freedom thus becomes the only criterion of moral value.

The pope is suggesting that life is a foundational value at the heart of every society. When it is threatened, the foundations of society as such are necessarily threatened. The culture of death is 'the value system that tolerates violation of human life and dignity of the weak wherever their protection demands limitations on the freedom of the strong'. This concerns not just the unborn or the terminally sick or the aged, but the rights of the poor, victims of war, migrants and refugees.

And the premiss of all these arguments is simple and simply stated: the human person possesses a dignity that is sacred and, therefore, all those conditions necessary to the realization and preservation of human dignity are due to all as human rights.

DEFEND MARRIAGE

The Ten Commandments take it for granted that we are constituted as human beings by our relationships: we are, in other words, social beings by nature. Some of these relationships we are born into – that of parents and family; others we inherit – social and civic relations, the state. Still others we create: the bonds of friendship and, in this commandment specifically, the particular friendship we call marriage.

The commandment to honour our parents emphasizes that our lives are gifts: the commandment not to kill innocent life enjoins us to reverence and respect that life, in ourselves and others, once received.

This commandment, though again expressed negatively – 'do not commit adultery' – promotes a positive value, namely, defend, protect and respect marriage. In the context of the commandments this injunction is a continuation of the commandment to value life in its entirety. Marriage here is regarded first and foremost as the well-spring of new life, the ideal and only safe environment within which new life can prosper.

But it is also part of the injunction to value life in another sense. It enjoins on us respect for the person: in this specific case the one flesh that two people who are married have become. It rests therefore on a conviction that this relationship, marriage, is unique in that two people have freely become identified with one another in such a manner as to admit of no rival or third party: an exclusive relationship at the level of their most intimate selves. The 'one flesh' of marriage, you might say, is a new creation and is to be accorded the profoundest respect, the same respect we have for another person.

That is the theory. Most people would agree that marriage is in crisis. Fewer people are marrying, divorce rates are rising and yet cohabitation has risen. Given these widely prevalent conditions, one could be forgiven for asking: *why* defend marriage? Why not let this ailing creature quietly go out of fashion and eventually die?

The perplexing feature of this seemingly dire situation is that second marriages account for a larger proportion than ever before of all marriages contracted. And why do people go on marrying and, indeed, enter into second and third and even more marriages? The triumph of hope over experience was Dr Johnson's description of second marriages. What drives people to marry? What's it for? Is it for everybody? And what are the alternatives?

Now in talking about marriage it is important to avoid two extremes, both of which trivialize it. One must avoid *both* downgrading *and* sentimentalizing it. Until recently, it was taken for granted that what distinguishes marriage from all other relationships is that it is a sexual relationship. And sexual relationships differ from all others in being, at least in principle, generative of new life. Before anything else and whatever else it is, sexual intercourse is the act of potential procreation. It was axiomatic until relatively recently, in other words, that marriage is inextricably bound up, in the normal course of things, with having children and a family. So we're talking about a unique relationship among all our relationships, in that this one involves that part of ourselves concerned with new life.

Now this is the heart of the matter. The arrangements made in different societies and throughout history to regulate and institutionalize this particular relationship have differed and still differ. But that it is a relationship that figures prominently in the way societies organize themselves arises from its reproductive aspects as well as from rights and property. It is, in other words, a public, communal, social reality, as much as it is a private, personal and intimate arrangement.

So why is marriage in crisis? There is no complete answer to this, obviously. One cannot help feeling that marriage suffers from the exaggerated expectations which people increasingly entertain of their lives in general. We are more prone that ever to believe uncritically the media myths of modern life; and the bliss of the perfect match and domestic harmony is certainly one of the most prevalent of these myths, as is the myth that we have a right to happiness. If difficulties in marriage occur that do not figure in the script, it must indicate that this is not right. And if it does not work out this time, you move on to the next. And so on.

Marriage is one of those things in life over which we cannot be half-hearted. If we do not give it our all, it will collapse around our heads or become a burden rather than a joy. Marriages are created, each of them individually by the two people involved: there is no blueprint. Weddings are easy, marriages take a lifetime's work. John Bayley said of his marriage to Iris Murdoch that after 40 years he finally felt they were beginning to get it together. Marriage is not an easy option, no matter how dewy-eyed the view of it in the glossy magazines. There is no greater joy than marital joy; but there is no more painful unhappiness than an unhappy marriage.

There is also a great deal of pressure, especially on young women, to regard marriage as their only course or, at least, the best course. This was once upon a time an economic necessity: but no longer. It is a great mistake to want to be married for its own sake but it is all too easy to slide into this mode of thinking through peer pressure and maternal anxiety. The only reason for marrying is that you want to marry this particular person: marriage is person specific. Only the right person will do. Marry in haste, repent at leisure.

So, you have finally found your Mr or Miss right. You have become the best of friends. And now you marry: freely, permanently and exclusively committing yourselves to each other, open to new life and open to an unknown but trust-filled and faithful future, whatever time brings, 'even to the edge of doom'. What does the Church say about this situation? The Church says that this situation is more than a human reality. This is a sacrament: that is, this relationship is imbued with the divine presence so that the continuing faithful relationship of you and your husband or wife is itself a manifestation of God's loving and providential presence in his creation, not just for you two, but for all of us. The sacrament is constituted by your mutual pledge, not by ecclesiastical *fiat* or ceremony or legal writ. In other words, *you* are the sacrament.

But not everybody is called to be married and marriage is not uniquely sacramental. Attaching importance to marriage must not lead us to downgrade the rich blessings and opportunities of the single life or the life of the Religious. God calls us all to be sacramental, to manifest his presence in creation in the calling to which, through circumstances and gifts and aptitudes, he invites us.

There is, of course, only one vocation to which we are all called: friendship, with one another in all its different forms, and with God, now and in the final and fulfilling communion of unending love in heaven.

PROPERTY, POVERTY AND RELATIONSHIPS

The concept of property has changed radically in recent times. Consider the fact that the corollary to the commandment about not coveting property is that one should not covet another's wife. Clearly, the association of these injunctions implies that a man's wife is his property. And indeed this was the case in the setting and at the time when these commandments were originally given. Or consider that until the end of the last century, stealing another's property was punishable by transportation to New South Wales in Australia – even if the property in question was a cotton shirt or a morsel of bread.

But consider also, in the other direction, how the concept of property has expanded. We uncontroversially think of publications and ideas as intellectual property, and we protect such things by means of trade marks and patents. The possibility of electronic theft and corporate crime has also made us more sensitive to the legitimate claim of ownership whose transgression affects us all in the form of the ever-expanding black economy and tax evasion.

Concepts of property and ownership have changed under the influence of a growing sense of interdependence across the globe, both economic and social, and a growing sensitivity to the plight of those chronically deprived of the necessities of life through no fault of their own. Social justice, in other words, has expanded our cherished notions of ownership and property.

Now one of the hidden treasures of Catholic doctrine is its social teaching. Its critics may accuse the Church of being preoccupied with sex in its moral theology, but no other Christian body has made a more vital contribution to social teaching in the modern world than the Catholic Church.

An interesting and topical example is the Common Market, the forerunner of the European Union. The framework of social theory which inspired Christian democrats in Europe as early as the 1920s to develop a Common Market and European integration, albeit with the prevention of future wars in mind, was taken from the social teaching of the Church. The founding fathers of the Common Market sought to drive a wedge between the individualism of liberals and the collectivism of socialists. One of their key principles was the notion of subsidiarity, which even now informs the workings of the European Union. This is the notion that the person, the family, and the smaller associations in society, whatever their function and purpose within a framework of just law, should be free of interference from larger associations, especially the state, unless the help of such organizations is needed for them to obtain their legitimate objectives.

Catholic social teaching first emerged in the nineteenth century in response to the conditions provoked by the Industrial Revolution. For the first time in human history there was a major civilization based on an industrial economy giving rise to an urbanized people. How was one to provide fair working and living conditions and just financial rewards for the non-property owning majority of wage-earners in towns and cities whose labour contributed vitally to the new wealth-creation process? Pope Leo XIII's social encyclical *Rerum Novarum* sought to answer such pressing new questions.

But sensitivity to the demands of social justice goes back to the Old Testament. The prophet Amos famously berates those who would exploit the poor and the weak. (Cf. Amos 6:4-7.) And the letter of James in the New Testament offers a swingeing attack on those who would show partiality to the rich.

> My brothers and sisters, do you with your acts of favoritism really believe in our glorious Lord Jesus Christ? For if a person with gold rings and in fine clothes comes into your assembly, and if a poor person in dirty clothes also comes in, and if you take notice of the one wearing fine clothes and you say, " Have a seat here, please," while to the one who is poor you say, "Stand there," or, "Sit at my feet", have you not made distinctions among yourselves and become judges with evil thoughts? Listen my beloved brothers and sisters. Has not God chosen the poor in the world to be rich in faith and to be heirs of the kingdom that he has promised to those who love him? But you have dishonoured the poor. (Jas. 2:1 – 6)

One of the chief contributions of Catholic social teaching has been to argue forcefully that care for the poor is not a matter of charity or philanthropy but justice. Many of the world's poor are poor not through sloth or fecklessness but through exploitation by other nations or even within individual nations between different sections of the same population. Catholic social teaching stresses that everybody has a right to share in the world's resources. To do nothing to ensure this or, even worse, to collude actively even if remotely through local and national economic practices is to transgress the seventh commandment.

But Catholic social teaching also defended the right of private property. So the Catholic Church set its face against Communism's invasion of privacy and its abolition of free enterprise. The right to private property, however, is not an absolute, according to Catholic social teaching. No individual or nation can amass the earth's goods to the point of causing deprivation of the basic necessities of life for others.

To seek a just distribution of the world's goods and resources, however, is in no way to encourage or endorse covetousness, the subject of the tenth commandment. This warns against that interior disposition which is the source of all manner of injustices: murder, violence, adultery, theft and lying. Covetousness is a form of egoism which our Lord warns us against: 'Take care! Be on your guard against all kinds of greed; for one's life does not consist in the abundance of possessions' (Luke 12:15). And John Calvin says that the point of this commandment is to banish from our hearts all desires contrary to love. The sole motive for action must be the good of our neighbour.

The great wisdom in all of this is endorsed by modern psychology. Excessive indulgence of our desires and appetites can easily become addictive, leading to compulsively destructive behaviour. Given unbridled and full rein, our appetites can enslave us. Like a drug, our need is never satisfied, our glass never full enough.

Perhaps the key to our understanding of property and ownership is given to us by the most basic fact of all: we are created and sustained in existence and are therefore utterly dependent on God for life itself, which is a gift entrusted to us. In an important sense, therefore, ownership is an illusion. How can we be said to own anything if, as is the case, we do not own even our lives? If, in truth, we own nothing, we are all poor. But it is a blessed poverty that makes us rich and well-placed to receive the gifts God bestows on us.

SAY WHAT YOU MEAN, AND MEAN WHAT YOU SAY

In the eighth commandment we are told that we must not bear false witness against our neighbour. This negative formulation, as in all the other commandments, enshrines a positive command: namely, seek, speak and respect the truth. But notice, this is not making a philosophical point. Rather it is enjoined upon us, as are all the other 'horizontal' commandments, in the context of relationships. And it stresses the indispensable role of truth-telling and truthful living for the maintenance of healthy and flourishing relationships, at all levels.

Negatively, it can be said to outlaw the whole gamut of ways in which we can destroy relationships: perjury, which fosters injustice; calumny, where we deprive another of their good name and standing by lying; detraction, where we destroy someone's character by depriving them of their legitimate privacy in the exposure of truths that someone else has no right to know; rash judgement, where we hastily and unjustifiably condemn or exclude or otherwise treat unfairly another person; bragging, where we project a false image of ourselves in order to achieve superiority over others; flattery, where we seek to manipulate others by encouraging an exaggerated and inflated view of themselves; servility and sycophancy, where we seek to mislead as to our true opinion in order fawningly to have the good opinion of others; and, finally, hypocrisy, whereby we project an image of ourselves which we know to be incongruent and blatantly incompatible with the truth about ourselves.

But the underlying injunction beneath all this is respect for the truth. Now seeking after truth permeates the whole of life. In our saner moments we know that anything less than the truth or reality ultimately lets us down. And this is not a mere matter of accuracy or precision, but authenticity: not an aspiration towards some abstract reality but a personal quality. But neither is it merely a quality of the individual: personal integrity and authenticity have a direct bearing on the complex structure of relationships, formal and informal, official and personal, which constitute our lives. Without truth there can be no trust, and without trust there can be no kind of satisfactory relationship, on any level.

But on a practical level, truth, both about the world and about ourselves, is elusive and today many doubt that there is such a thing as truth, other than the socially conditioned, culturally created, pragmatically useful agreements that are impermanent and relative. With telling insight and clarity, such thinkers as Richard Rorty suggest that the notion of objective truth is inextricably tied to the notion of a Creator God and, since this latter notion has disappeared from view, so there is no justification for the former notion. It is a central tenet of post-modernism that we do not have and cannot have access to any extra-linguistic and extra-human meanings and truth. Truth is human, socially produced, historically developed, plural and changing. The notion of an ultimate truth is incompatible with the fluid and transient nature of language: 'the world is an argument that never gets settled.'[25]

Now there is intellectual sleight of hand going on here. In making this point, the relativist is *either* claiming some truth about all linguistically expressed human thought: and if so, the performance contradicts the content, namely that all assertions are language and culture-bound and do not connect up with reality. *Or*, if this is not the case, then his own view is itself relativized. And if this is so, why worry? We can go on making claims and assertions that aspire to the truth. The relativist programme constitutes the self-sabotage of intellectual enquiry as such: the claim that we have no access to objective truth is a recipe for intellectual suicide. We need not be intimidated.

But given that there is indeed such a thing as truth, what are the factors that inhibit our seeking and speaking it? Clearly fear is one powerful factor: fear not just of being found out or ridiculed but also fear of being known. So one way of respecting and seeking the truth is the creation and maintenance of climates of genuine trust in which people are enabled to feel safe and surrounded by good will. Dietrich Bonhoeffer spoke of the necessity within any community of what he called 'the ministry of holding one's tongue'. By this he meant not merely refraining from uttering untruths but also from uttering truths that tend to destroy the climate of trust.

Now the point being made here is not that we should indulge in dissimulation or duplicity, but that respect for the truth entails both discretion as much as honesty. People have a right to expect us to place the best interpretation on their words and deeds, just as they have a right to assume our good will.

But equally there are also truths about us and everybody else that are not for general release or universal dissemination. The need for truths to be known is always context-related and respect for the person entails and requires that we maintain respect for the boundaries each individual decides to establish. St Thomas More spoke of the 'poison dart of murmuring', the destructive habit of half-truth articulated for entertainment or the relief of boredom, at the cost of another's good name or place in a community.

In one sense, this commandment takes us back to the beginning where we are told to worship God and God alone, since he is not only the source of truth, but the Truth, the ultimate and all-encompassing truth. The loss or, even worse, the denial of this truth, therefore, is a denial of all truth. And the greatest act of respect for truth is the witness to this Truth.

Martyrdom is dramatically spoken of by one of the early Fathers of the Church as 'the truth written in blood'. To witness to this truth with one's life is to attain to the absolute truth. But we align ourselves with the ultimate truth even now when we strive for harmony between heart, hand and head, by saying what we mean and meaning what we say. And this is not only a matter of speech but also deed: 'What I do is me', says the Jesuit poet, Gerard Manley Hopkins.

PART III

The Seven Deadly Sins

THE FIRST DEADLY SIN: PRIDE

Catholics are frequently charged with being obsessed with sin and racked with guilt: what was instilled into us, it is often alleged, was the fear of God not the love of God. Well, whether the charge sticks and just how you would judge its truth is difficult to say. My impression is that whatever truth there is in the charge has more to do with climate than conscience and is more common among northern European Catholics than Mediterranean ones. Nevertheless, to devote a whole section of this essay to the subject of sin – and not just sin, but deadly sins – might seem to lend credence to this caricature of the sin-obsessed Catholic.

In my view, it is more true to say that we Catholics are obsessed, not with sin, but with forgiveness. And if you do not find comfort and encouragement in that, then you are very special indeed. Only a sick man appreciates the skill of the surgeon and you can appreciate Good News only if you are in need of it. And only a person at home and familiar with the contours of our human nature is in a position to appreciate the importance of forgiveness.

Now one thing that can be said about Catholicism is that it is not squeamish about human nature. Various versions of dualism have sought to escape the more untidy aspects and features of human nature and various early heresies tried to sanitize the picture presented by Christianity: so, for instance, it was claimed by some that Christ did not really die, that he was not really human and so was not involved in all the messy business of physical and material existence. Again, it was claimed by some very early on in Christianity that the goal before us was to escape from and be free of the physical aspects of our nature, allowing our purified souls to soar heavenwards, unhindered by the dead weight of the body.

All these were and are heresies and distortions of the Christian message. We are bodies *and* souls in a unity: we cannot and must not neglect one in favour of the other, in either direction. The head apart from the heart is as dangerous as the heart apart from the head. We are a complex of the physical, spiritual, intellectual, emotional and affective, and virtue resides, among other things, in a balance and harmony among all these elements.

Again, in our own day, the nineteenth-century ideology of progress lingers on in the illusion of human perfectibility by effort alone, and this despite all the evidence to the contrary. In matters of the utmost importance, we more often seem to be moving backwards. And yet endless numbers of popular magazine articles and self-help books hold out hope of perfect happiness and offer a million different ways of smoothing out the wrinkles in our natures and making ourselves presentable both to ourselves and the world.

In the midst of all the millennium junketings just past, with their fatuous posturings and proud boasts about human achievement, it passed unnoticed that we have just staggered to the end of the bloodiest and most brutal century in history. Having witnessed the horror of the Holocaust and the mass murder of millions in Soviet Russia, Communist China and Pol Pot's Cambodia; having seen the near successful attempts at genocide in Rwanda and the ferocious internecine wars in Northern Ireland, the Balkans, Palestine, Chechnya and Indonesia, it is exceedingly difficult to take seriously any notion of human perfectiblity or the Enlightenment dream of an earthly paradise. You need look no further than your television screen to realize that there seems to be something profoundly and dangerously wrong with us, a flaw that cannot be wished or thought away, an ineradicable sickness of soul. And whatever we see on our screens is only what we find in our own hearts from time to time, only writ large.

Now Christianity's traditional way of accounting for these unmistakable symptoms of dis-ease is the doctrine of original sin. This is an account that points to the originating energy of all sin but it starts from the universal human experience of both individuals and societies that things are not now as they originally were. This teaching is not meant to depress us or convince us of our worthlessness; on the contrary, it offers hope by shedding light on our condition. If we are unable to confront and acknowledge the problem, Christianity's answer makes no sense.

Now we are adepts at circumlocution and subterfuge when it comes to the uncomfortable subject of sin: we cast blame on environment, genetics, parental hang-ups, and a whole host of other factors. But all these strategies for evasion leave us dissatisfied. If we fail to confront this aspect of our nature, we see only half of the truth about ourselves. Sin, nevertheless, is only part of the story and original sin does not tell the whole or the most important part of the tale. If there is something irreducibly wrong with us, there is also something inescapably and stubbornly right about us. We have been created in the image and likeness of God and that image has not been and can never be completely obliterated. G. K. Chesterton once said that the only mystery more puzzling than the question of evil is the question of good.

And so talk of the Seven Deadly Sins is intended not to discourage but to discover solidarity in realism about the human nature we all share and the flaws therein in which we also all share. Ignorance of the possible pitfalls and obstacles in any project we undertake and blithe optimism about our unaided capacity to deal with them will inevitably leave us unprepared when we come up against problems. The Seven Deadly Sins were a traditional topic for preachers during Lent until relatively recently. Though the fashion for preaching about them has declined, there's been no noticeable decline in our enthusiasm for the Seven Deadly Sins themselves.

The list of Seven Deadly Sins – originally they were called Capital Sins because they were thought to be the source of all others – has a long pedigree stretching back as far as early monasticism in the East. Nevertheless, we hear relatively little of them now. And even if we have not exactly forgotten them, most of us, as Dorothy L. Sayers once remarked, cannot remember what the other six are.[26] This memory lapse is reflected, as Sayers said in the same place, in the fact that someone may be known to exhibit in his life every vice and character defect known to man, but the catch-all designation 'immoral' will be attached to him or her by the tabloids if and only if he falls into the one deadly sin we all remember.

Let's remind ourselves of the names of the Seven Deadly Sins; or, at least, the names of the other six. It was again Dorothy L.

Sayers who, with brilliant insight, first suggested that the seven should be divided up into the three disreputable but warm-hearted sins; and the four respectable but cold-hearted sins. In the first category are Lust, Wrath and Gluttony. In the other category are Covetousness, Envy, Sloth and, the darkest and root of all the others, Pride.

These last four were 'cold-hearted' because they were sins of the spirit (and sins of the spirit, says St Thomas, are, other things being equal, more likely to be graver than sins of the flesh). They are called 'respectable' because they easily masquerade as virtue, even unwittingly. Our Lord, of course, rebukes the warm-hearted sins, but in a general way. He reserves his most stringent reproof, however, for the cold-hearted deadly sins. And, more often than not, he has got the poor old Pharisees in his sights.

Now, of the seven deadly sins Aquinas and many others have always thought that pride – *superbia* – is the deadliest. Lust 'the expense of spirit in a waste of shame', as Shakespeare has it, may be the most conspicuous symptom of original sin, but pride is the original sin itself: that is, the sin of trying to displace God, of trying to be God yourself. It is, in other words, a form of idolatry. Pride sets us up as our own judges: it suggests that we are sufficient for all our needs. And pride actually converts virtue into deadly sin precisely by misattributing its source to ourselves, rather than God. Remember our Lord tells the parable of the Publican and the Pharisee 'to some who trusted in themselves that they were righteous'. The disturbing thing about pride is that it attacks us, not in our weaknesses, but in our strengths. This is why it's pre-eminently the sin of the talented and the gifted and why it does more damage than all the sins of weakness put together.

Pride, then, is the deadliest of all the deadly sins. It turns us away from God and makes us the centre of the universe. It is thus the sin of the solipsist, leading us inexorably into the lonely wasteland of isolation. It engenders the cold illusion of self-sufficiency and it leads, ultimately paradoxically, to its twin sister, despair.

THE SECOND DEADLY SIN: SLOTH

Another traditional name for the deadly sin of sloth is accidie, from the medieval Latin for 'listlessness'. This older word catches a key feature of this condition: sloth consists in a profoundly debilitating lassitude affecting the soul itself, a weakening of our powers of judgement and distinction and engagement. Sloth is precisely the sin of self-centred disengagement in which we are turned in on ourselves and cut off from every other consideration. As such, it is the ultimate outcome of a million acts of selfishness that, singly, seem insignificant but jointly and over time coalesce into a conspiracy of isolation and solitary self-preoccupation. And, as in the case of pride, sloth leads inexorably to the dreaded state of despair.

Sloth is the condition of the spiritual sleepwalker: it 'believes in nothing, cares for nothing, seeks to know nothing, interferes with nothing, enjoys nothing, loves nothing, hates nothing, finds purpose in nothing, lives for nothing, and only remains alive because there is nothing it would die for'.[27] In other words, the soul is empty, the heart is empty, and eventually the brain is drained of its vigour. Many writers have suggested that sloth accompanies all the other deadly sins and manifests itself only when the others have wreaked their havoc and done their deadly damage.

Now I said that the peculiar feature of the four cold-hearted but respectable deadly sins — Pride, Sloth, Envy and Covetousness – is that they easily masquerade as virtues. By this I do not mean only that those in their grip dissimulate and pretend to be virtuous. I mean also that the world frequently congratulates and applauds those whose lives are guided by these deadly conditions of the soul. Pride, for instance, is translated by the world into strength of character, self-sufficiency, independence, ambition, determination to do well, good opinion and popularity.

Sloth masquerades under two names, one of which is the chief virtue of liberal democracy and the other is a prevailing temptation to which modern man is particularly prone. The first is tolerance, the second is workaholism. Tolerance, of course, is a virtue. But when tolerance becomes an end in itself, an ideological principle rather than a practical requirement of social existence, then it is a dangerous threat to rational and reasonable existence. The underlying philosophical rationale for this ideological view goes by the name of 'subjectivism' and the arena within which it manifests itself most dangerously is that of ethics.

Now it is a self-evident, uncontroversial, and perfectly acceptable canon of contemporary liberalism that 'everybody is entitled to his own view' and 'no segment of the community has the right to impose its moral view on another'. However, subjectivism proposes much more than this perfectly acceptable principle of democratic freedom. It holds that there is no such thing as objective truth and therefore no test or criterion of truth. The subjectivist holds, instead, that all opinions are true for those who hold them. Your ethical viewpoint and opinion depends on the kind of person you are, your preferences, your background and temperament. Instead of objective truth, to be discovered and arrived at, there is only what you decide.

As such, moral subjectivism is a major threat to the intelligibility of ethical reflection as well as an obstacle to actual reflection in practice, especially in the realm of public debate about social policy. But it is also a serious threat on another level: if nothing is objectively right or wrong, good or bad in any absolute sense, then it is a small step to the view that nothing matters at all objectively; and then we are not far from the destructive moral and personal nihilism that corrodes the very foundations of a reasonable human existence. And for this, read sloth.

Now the much-vaunted virtue of tolerance clearly has its limits, both practical and logical. The very existence of the institution of law would make no sense, were this not the case. And in practice, who would not find repugnant human sacrifice, child-abuse and matricide. The repugnance here is instructive and we ignore it at our peril. The 'yuk' factor still counts. Of course, in practice, nobody actually thinks that morality is just a matter of everybody's subjective opinion, because human life simply cannot be carried on at all without a wide measure of moral agreement. (Even in the Mafia, people have to have standards that they take for granted.)[28]

But, as we saw earlier, there are logical problems. There can be no such thing as absolute tolerance: it would, as it were, cancel itself out since it is a contradiction in terms. The principle of tolerance, undergirded by subjectivism, cannot hold, on the one hand, that each person is free to choose his own moral principles or that no group has the right to impose its moral views on others and, at the same time, hold that tolerance is obligatory or even preferable. That we ought to be tolerant is itself a moral judgement and, as such, the subjectivist must say that this too is only a personal feeling or preference which does not necessarily oblige you if you feel otherwise. Tolerance, taken to this extreme, must be tolerant of intolerance. The idea of absolute tolerance is clearly incoherent.

Finally, subjectivism is the resort of us all on occasion when faced with unwelcome conclusions or difficulty. We are all capable of finding within ourselves 'an inarticulate private self which is held accountable to nobody' when it suits us.[29] And all too often we grace this 'self' with the name 'conscience', thus affording ourselves an inaccessible source of moral decision-making which needs no defence and claims absolute rights beyond the reach of reason. For 'conscience' here, read 'special pleading'.

Sloth or spiritual inactivity, is often concealed by the other feature of modernity: namely, workaholism or activism. We think that if we are fully occupied and busy rushing about doing things, we cannot be suffering from sloth. But energetic, fervid, external activity is perfectly consistent with sloth. And this is where the other deadly sins provide a cover: gluttony offers the distraction that goes with wanting to *do* everything, *be* everywhere, *see* everything and not miss out on anything; but within we are without life. Covetousness provides us with the motivation for diligence in order not to miss out on opportunities for gathering to ourselves more and more and making headway in our business and career affairs. Envy motivates us to devote energies to endless tittle-tattle and worse, seeking to undermine good names so as to appear in a better light ourselves. Wrath justifies loud condemnation of those who do not achieve our own high standards or who remind us of our own secret failings. And lust engenders its own prodigious energies in pursuit of the passing moment of pleasure at the cost of personal respect and genuine concern for another person.

Sloth and emptiness go together. Sloth puts a brake on thinking: it persuades us that it's no use trying to understand or learn or improve our grasp of anything. Stupidity is not our fault and thinking gets us nowhere. Once convinced of this we are vulnerable to ideologies and totalitarianisms and tyrannies of various kinds, and not only of the easy-to-detect political variety. As with pride, so with sloth: it eventually spawns all the other deadly sins. But, in practice, its closest ally is envy.

THE THIRD DEADLY SIN: ENVY

Of all the deadly sins, envy is without doubt the most insidious. Its chameleon-like character enables it to masquerade as virtue more effectively than all the others. Envy is so universally pervasive that it goes unnoticed by most, and yet, almost uniquely among the deadly sins, it can assume social and political forms that are far more damaging than its manifestation in the life of an individual.

Envy emerges early. Even little children display envy. When a child sees that someone has something he or she wants its first instinct is to snatch it away from them. The objects of envy obviously change as we grow, yet the nature of envy remains.

What makes envy so unattractive is that, at its root, it hates to see other people happy. And this dark and sinister tendency hidden in our nature is all the more invisible because the virtues and values whose form envy assumes are the indisputable shibboleths of enlightened, liberal society: namely, rights, justice and equality. These noble, altruistic aspirations, these building blocks of the brave new world, are frequently paraded as the justification for acts of outright if concealed envy.

Envy begins in churlishness and asks 'Why haven't I got what others more fortunate than I have?' But it eventually arrives at a completely different interrogation: 'Why should anybody have such good fortune, if I cannot?' The problem is that this mean-spirited desire to bring everybody down to the same level may easily assume the outward form of egalitarian austerity. It can be concealed under the guise of apparently enlightened social policy. But under pretence of justice and fairness, envy is the most destructive of the deadly sins because, focused entirely on self, it would rather see us all suffer together rather than have anybody happier than itself. At its best, envy is a ruthless self-promoter, using any means to attain its desired goal; at worst it is a potent destructive force, prepared to dismantle and set back anything it cannot itself possess.

One particularly destructive form which envy takes in the lives of individuals is possessiveness. It wants others to be absorbed entirely in me, seeking for nothing outside of this particular relationship. This can happen in friendship, but it is at its worst in marriage. Envy is at the root of that paralysing suffocation that can infect a marriage, where one partner claims as a right that nothing should be allowed to distract the other person from devoting undivided attention to the other. And if this leads, as it inevitably does, to the profoundest unhappiness in the marriage, then so be it. Envy is more content that all should be equally unhappy.

But beyond the private confines of marriage, envy's destructive ways are evident in its inability to take pleasure in the gifts and achievements of all others, even those closest to one. Instead, such good fortune on the part of others produces in the envious person feelings of permanent inferiority. The only respite available for such uncomfortable feelings is sneering and derision; all, of course, under a show of interested and constructive criticism. And again, when this happens in the public forum of social policy, envy seeks to nullify and render worthless any privilege or adornment others may have, under the guise of supporting equal rights.

Envy, then, is the sin of those who cannot see what they have because they spend all their time eyeing what everybody else has got. But one reason why envy is so intractable and difficult to deal with is precisely that its call for justice is always plausible and hard to criticize. Those acting from envy are likely to have the support of the generous and fair-minded, and those who have the temerity to suggest that envy is the motivating impulse behind such calls for equality can easily be accused of oppression, inertia, and callous insensitivity towards the poor. The social and political ramifications of envy, therefore, are vast and the world can be held to ransom by rampant envy.

'The politics of envy' is a commonly heard phrase these days but politics based on envy spells disaster for us all and helps to distort our understanding of the goals of social existence. Consider how rooted in our Western consciousness the notion of the market now is. Everything is a commodity and everyone is a customer. Nothing is valued in and for itself, not even education and knowledge. Everything is valued for the profit it yields even where this is translated into the anodyne but misleading phrases such as 'improving the quality of life', and making a 'contribution to society'. Knowledge and education and all those involved in it now have a market value. The power of individuals is rated on the basis of what bargain they are in a position to strike. Even the family is now valued, if at all, as an economic unit. Nothing, in other words, has intrinsic value: such a notion is denied and derided as the breeder of inequality. And if, as has happened, the ills of society are understood in exclusively financial and utilitarian terms, then the goods of society and the life of the individual also are reduced to the same level.

One particularly insidious disguise assumed by envy is righteous railing against hypocrisy. Now we all agree that hypocrisy is one of the ugliest growths bred always in the warm shade of virtue. In the Gospels, it is the one failing for which our Lord reserves his ire. But envy rather than the love of justice is often the moving force behind the desire to root out and expose hypocrisy. Envy is the ally, not the enemy, of hypocrisy and the pleasure taken in revelations of the private weaknesses of public figures is usually a sign that envy not honesty is at work.

But envy is not satisfied with rooting out the parasitic growths around something good. Far from weeding the garden to restore its health, envy is satisfied only when the garden is laid waste. Because envy is offended by virtue it cannot bear to admire or respect, and it knows nothing of gratitude and joy in the good fortune of others.

St Augustine thought envy was the diabolical sin.[30] And Gregory the Great says that 'From envy are born hatred, detraction, calumny, joy caused by the misfortune of a neighbour, and displeasure caused by his prosperity.'[31] The Book of Wisdom (2: 24) says that death entered the world through the devil's envy. But its very plausibility as a worker in the cause of justice and equality conceals its deadly poison. Remember T. S. Eliot in *Murder in the Cathedral*: 'The last temptation is the greatest treason, to do the right deed for the wrong reason.'[32]

Envy is the saddest of all sins: it deprives us of peace of mind and leads inexorably to the desolation of irredeemable joylessness. But as with all sin so with envy in particular: the one who generates this poison is its final victim. Like a moral cancer it burrows deep into the very well-springs of all our activity, emotion and thought and lays waste all that is good. It is the most debilitating of sins and, more explicitly than any other, it displays the essential characteristic of all sin: it is self-consuming and self-destructive.

THE FOURTH DEADLY SIN: AVARICE

The last of the cold-hearted, respectable deadly sins is covetousness or avarice: greed for the things of this world, especially, but not exclusively, material things. This is the sin which, above all others, breeds injustice and all manner of conflicts between both individuals and nations. If envy is the ruling sin of the 'have-nots', avarice is the dominating sin of the 'haves' who, insanely but unsurprisingly, want even more.

Possession and ownership and the power arising from them can be as addictive as any drug, and it is an undeniable fact of experience that if you are inordinately attached to something, you can never have enough of it. The need to have more quickly becomes a compulsion that wantonly elbows aside every other consideration. But this sin, which can all too easily overtake a person's life, is rooted, like all sin, in an illusion: in this case, it is the illusion of ownership.

Avarice is versatile. As the sin can manifest itself both in the life of the individual and the life of society, so it can masquerade as both the virtue of thrift and the virtue of enterprise. (Were not these the ruling virtues of Thatcherism?) But thrift is itself an ambiguous virtue. We only half admire it because it can all too easily become that most unattractive pseudo-virtue, parsimony. Thrift, nevertheless, as we all know from experience, is often a necessity. The point is that thrift is never, or should never be, an end in itself. We fast today in order to feast or even just feed tomorrow. Parsimony is precisely thrift for its own sake: a joyless preoccupation with detail and security, usually focused exclusively on one's own needs. When this happens, thrift is a cover for avarice. And remember, you do not have to have much to be avaricious about it: you just have to have bought in to the illusion that you can have anything at all, the illusion of ownership.

The social virtue which conceals avarice and covetousness is enterprise: and this, more than anything else, according to our social engineers and enlightened politicians, whether New Right or New Labour, characterizes the ideal culture and society towards which we are encouraged to aspire. We are taught to value the entrepreneur, the risk-taking, energetic, competitive spirit that builds, builds, builds, increasing stock and profits, satisfying the shareholder, expanding the business, creating prosperity, etc., etc. But, as we are warned by investment management advertisements, our investments may go up or down. For as long as we share the profits of enterprise we are well-pleased and prepared to overlook how the rise has taken place. But when the downward turn comes and our profit turns to loss, then we point the finger at covetousness overreaching itself in the form of greed. Greed is translated into 'business efficiency' if the business is going well and we are sharing in the profits; but it is plain, old-fashioned avarice when our shares drop through the floor.

Now if envy is the saddest sin, avarice is the silliest, because it trades on an illusion, a sleight of hand. Concerning material goods and riches, there are in the Gospels some startling and arresting sayings of our Lord. Perhaps the most startling of all is when he says that 'It is easier for a camel to pass through the eye of a needle than for a rich man to enter the kingdom of heaven'. But there is also the first of the beatitudes: Blessed are the poor (in Luke) and the poor in spirit (in Matthew). In both these sayings our Lord seems to suggest an incompatibility between prosperity and success (of whatever kind) in this world and prosperity in the world to come. The saying about the camel and the eye of a needle is an instance of a familiar Semitic literary device, hyperbole. You simply cannot get a camel through the eye of a needle: you simply cannot get into heaven if you are rich. The real question then concerns what it is to be rich and what it is to be poor. And this is where the illusion of ownership comes in.

The truth is that we are all poor, because none of us owns anything, in reality. We do not own even our physical existence: it is given to us, and it will be taken from us. So the only important question is: are we prepared to acknowledge that we are poor, and live accordingly? Or do we go on suffering the illusion of ownership, and live as if all we had was our own?

Our Lord says in the Sermon on the Mount: 'Do not store up for yourselves treasures on earth.' (Matt. 6:19) We should not, because we cannot. It is, in the strictest sense, unrealistic. It simply does not work. Even if we manage to preserve our goods from moths, rust and burglars, we cannot preserve them from ourselves, simply because we cannot preserve ourselves to enjoy them. We have no final hold on our lives: even less on anything less than our very lives.

In another story he told, our Lord ridiculed, pointed out the silliness of, a man who built himself enormous barns to hoard his ever-increasing crops: and that very night, he was visited by death. 'You Fool! This very night your life is being demanded of you. And the things you have prepared, whose will they be?' (Luke 12:16ff.) The moral is that, in this life, we cannot possess or own anything because we cannot and do not possess or own even our lives. And so the attempt to catch things and hold on to them and increase them: the drive to say, 'Right, that's mine, I've got it!' is fundamentally misconceived. It is to be led up the garden path: to nowhere, in other words.

But the pernicious illusion of possession has become an obsession of fallen man. And yet, of course, we all know its futility, from our own experience of possessiveness. Possessiveness is, without doubt, the greatest destroyer of relationships. One sure way of losing friendship of any kind is to try to hang on to it too tightly. Friendship can be enjoyed only as it is constantly received as a gift which is ever new.

And that is the antidote for avarice. Only a poor person can appreciate a gift and only one who loves can see through the gift to the giver. Paradoxically, you can have the most important things in life only if you do not treat them as though they belonged to you. Only if you see everything as a gift can you enjoy anything at all in this world. And if you see all as gift, then the two virtues that will characterize you are gratitude and generosity: the two most attractive virtues and, even from a secular, psychological point of view, two of the most positive and life-enhancing attributes. Generosity, and gratitude are the opposite of avarice and, by definition, they are reckless, uncalculating, joyous and life-giving.

But, finally, the reason why it is so important for us to see through the illusion of possessing and possession is that the only thing worth possessing is utterly beyond all possessing. We are made for God, the source of everything, and, ultimately, nothing else will satisfy us. In the light of this, it is just plain silly to hold on to anything less or to invest our total trust in anything less.

When St Francis of Assisi stripped himself naked before the

whole of Assisi he was making a wholly positive gesture. He was dramatically expressing his conviction that he was the richest of all men, that he was possessed by God. This is the meaning of his declaration, which is still the motto of the Franciscan Order he founded: *Deus meus et omnia*. My God and my All. The virtue (and the vow) of poverty are not about having nothing, but about having everything, as a gift, and settling for nothing less. Avarice, the silliest of the deadly sins, is about blindness to the abundance which is already ours.

THE FIFTH DEADLY SIN: GLUTTONY

So we leave the cold-hearted but respectable deadly sins, and come, at last, to the disreputable but warm-hearted ones – Gluttony, Wrath, and Lust. While the cold-hearted sins take effort and concentration, and can easily masquerade as virtues, the warm-hearted sins arise from an all-too-familiar weakness that at least has the virtue of being obvious and apparent, with little room for hypocrisy and dissimulation. Hence the epithet 'disreputable' which attaches to these sins: they are, plainly and without concealment, just what they are. The warm-hearted deadly sins have in common that they all concern appetites that are, in themselves, good and directed to good things, but which can easily be distorted and disordered, directed towards inappropriate goals.

The first is gluttony. When we think of gluttony, the image that springs immediately to mind is the consumption of gargantuan amounts of food and drink in a Bacchanalian orgy of indulgence and debauchery. Now there is no doubt that this kind of behaviour did not die out with the decadence of the declining Roman Empire: there is still plenty of this kind of thing about.

But we may feel, with just a hint of self-satisfied superiority, that this does not apply to us. For one thing we cannot afford to pig ourselves at the rich man's table. For another, even if we could, we are far too sophisticated and refined to indulge in such vulgar excess. Or, so we think, in the absence of opportunity.

But gluttony is much more subtle and insidious and, therefore, more widespread that this vulgar caricature. The sin of gluttony is the sin of excess, leading to disproportionate indulgence and, though it concerns primarily food, it can and does extend to practically everything, including experiences of various kinds and, indeed, life itself. Gluttony or greed, to give it its more earthy name, is primarily an attitude and disposition, a state of mind, a condition of the heart, whose effects extend far beyond the private life of the individual.

Greed is the cause of much that afflicts the world as a whole at many different levels. It is, for example, at the root of that conspicuous consumerism which so clearly characterizes the Western world: the culture of more and more, and its corollary, more and more waste. In the immediate post-war period, for instance, with the rise of the welfare state, talk of raising living standards unambiguously referred to those conditions necessary for a healthy and secure existence: a decent supply of food, clothes, shelter, medical care and education for every citizen. But this entirely reasonable objective has now been overtaken in the prosperous West by an altogether different set of expectations. Needs have been replaced by wants, and blind wants as opposed to reasonable needs are the moving force behind much that fuels our Western economy, both its alleged successes and its all too obvious failures.

Again, many of the apparently intractable problems experienced in Western efforts to aid Third World countries are far more than logistical; as indeed are the many ecological problems requiring urgently to be addressed. These global problems are rooted in entrenched attitudes and practices that stem from a level of indulgence which satisfies the want of luxuries rather than the need of necessities.

Now there is in all of us a tendency to convert wants into needs. This is the standard rationalization we use to justify all manner of things. It is the old and familiar distinction between good reasons and real reasons for doing something. We in the First World have come more and more to regard luxuries as necessities and, as a result, the machinery of mass production toils incessantly to provide the unnecessary for a few, while the many lack what is necessary for a civilized existence at best and survival at worst. In such a situation, production and consumption become a vicious circle.

The irresistible lure of sales is a salutary reminder of how easily need is replaced by whim and want. The sales are a vital aspect of mass production: unless stock can be cleared, further production is blocked and profit inhibited. At sales time we are persuaded to acquire what neither we nor the producer needs. The result is that our lives become evermore cluttered with the detritus of yesterday's luxuries. This is part of the reason why we have become a throw-away culture, in which nothing is worth mending or repairing because nothing has intrinsic value. Everything is repeatable and reproducible and nothing lasts. We are the victims of our own sophistication.

Or consider our vulnerability to the immense power advertising has to disturb reasonable contentment by means of flattery and fear; and how easily the advertisers' appeal to every ignoble instinct manages so easily to distract us from reason and moderation. This irrational desire for more and more of whatever is on offer goes deep and can touch any and every experience. As such it is remorseless and relentless in the pursuit of its ultimately unattainable goal because, by definition, it can never be satisfied. Even entirely worthy and, indeed, noble objectives and aspirations can engage us in a disordered way, resulting in that restless impatience which so easily rids us of peace of mind and contentment. Never was Aristotle's wise dictum 'All things in moderation' more applicable than now.

Most of us would agree that greed in an individual, in ourselves and others, is one of the most unattractive characteristics. As of gluttony and greed, so with the other warm-hearted sins: what they seek is no sooner had than hated; self-serving gives way to self-loathing. In the public perception they are disreputable, but even in private realization they lessen and undermine self-respect. Their irrationality is almost palpable, even in their execution.

And this marks the distinction between the warm-hearted and the cold-hearted sins. The warm-hearted sins are distortions of virtues rather than their counterfeit versions. Greed seeks something that is good, but it seeks it in inappropriate and disproportionate excess. It is a positive instinct turned in upon itself. Greed or gluttony is the outcome when a generous, carefree, spontaneous love of life and the good things of life is overtaken by indiscipline and excess. The spontaneity of good-natured joy and cheerfulness are overtaken by anxiety and fearfulness, leading to the lean and hungry look of the schemer and calculator, aiming always to maximize consumption.

The warm-hearted sins are weaknesses arising from strengths, but they make us vulnerable to those whose lives are dominated by the cold-hearted sins. In particular, greed makes us vulnerable to the avaricious. The avaricious speculator, for instance, will more often than not have made his millions on the backs of the greedy.

But, unattractive as it may be, greed is a most human failing, arising more from fear and folly than grim determination to come out on top. It sits easily with lack of trust and anxiety, the fear of missing out or being left behind, as much as uncontrolled appetites. In the Gospels, our Lord sympathetically shakes his head at the way we needlessly fret and worry about all manner of things. And perhaps these are the words most accurately addressed to what is at the root of greed and gluttony in all its forms.

> Therefore, I tell you, do not worry about your life, what you will eat and drink, or about your body, what you will wear. Is not life more than food, and the body more than clothing? Look at the birds of the air: they neither sow nor reap, nor gather into barns, and yet your heavenly Father feeds them. Are you not of more value than they? And can any of you by worrying add a single hour to your span of life? And why do you worry about clothing? Consider the lilies of the field, how they grow: they neither toil nor spin, yet I tell you, even Solomon in all his glory was not clothed like one of these. But if God so clothes the grass of the field, which is alive today and tomorrow is thrown into the oven, will he not much more clothe you - you of little faith? Therefore, do not worry, saying, "What will we eat?" or "What will we drink?" or "What will we wear?" for it is the Gentiles who strive for all these things: and indeed your heavenly father knows that you need all these things. But strive first for the kingdom of God and his righteousness, and all these things will be given to you as well.
>
> So do not worry about tomorrow, for tomorrow will bring worries of its own. Today's trouble is enough for today.
>
> (Matt. 6:25–34)

THE SIXTH DEADLY SIN: WRATH

'It is the mark of the virtuous man to be angry at injustice.' This comment of St Thomas Aquinas reminds us that the deadly sin of anger or wrath must not be confused with that justified outburst of indignation on behalf of those unjustly treated or dealt with. Of course, this flash of anger must give way to considered strategies and reasonable effort to remove the injustice: of itself, the anger leads nowhere, except to provide emotional momentum for the real work for justice. Nevertheless, as was evident when Jesus himself overturned the money-changers' tables in the Temple, it is perfectly natural and reasonable when confronted by wrong to react sharply. In this sense, we all need to learn how to manage anger so that it does not get in the way of positive action.

Quite unlike this natural response on the level of the emotions is the deadly sin of wrath. More than an emotional and momentary reaction, wrath takes the form of a disposition, engaging the will and the mind as well as the emotions, aimed at harm to another, usually as a means of revenge and retaliation. As such, it is accompanied by deliberation and forethought, in which actions are marshalled for maximal impact on the object of one's wrath.

Anger of this destructive kind can arise from mismanaged anger of the justified and constructive kind, in which repeated and pointless outbursts give way to a settled and sustained attitude of mind rather than leading us energetically to seek our disadvantaged neighbour's good. In some, such anger comes to characterize a person's outlook and responses, colouring their view of everybody and every situation. When we call somebody 'quick-tempered' or irascible, we usually mean that they see offence where none is intended or that their reaction is out of all proportion to the perceived hurt.

Perhaps of all the deadly sins, anger is the one upon which psychology has cast most light, enabling us to draw distinctions we otherwise might have failed to make. For example, displacement is an unconscious mechanism in which an individual represses justified anger arising reasonably from a situation in which the person unjustly treated is helpless to do anything in self-defence, either through fear or constraint. That 'buried' and forgotten anger then resurfaces and is directed unreasonably and inexplicably at all manner of situations and persons. It is this that can be at the root of chronic irascibility and, of course, where this is the case, culpability is minimized if not obviated in the individual. What is needed here is medical help not moral exhortation.

Again, one who suffers from irascible intolerance of others' failings is frequently giving vent to anger and intolerance directed at themselves. Precisely those things, usually weaknesses and failings, we find ugly in ourselves, we attack in others; all the while failing to notice the presence of exactly the same imperfections in ourselves. It is instructive and sometimes shocking to make a written list of those things we most dislike in a particular person. Long before we arrive at a complete dossier, we will more often than not begin to recognize a far more familiar collection of characteristics: namely, our own.

But as all the other deadly sins are examples of love misplaced or excessive love, so this too, when its roots are not unconscious and therefore partially beyond our control, often arises from a misplaced concern for our own welfare. And the single most potent factor that has encouraged this in the modern world is assertion of individual rights as an absolute value.

That there are inalienable natural rights cannot be doubted and the acknowledgement of such rights is manifestly one of modernity's chief achievements. Medieval thinkers concerned themselves less with rights than with duties and obligations owed to the king or God. But since the seventeenth century the question of natural rights has increasingly engaged the attention of political and legal thinkers. It rapidly became a commonly held conviction that it was the first duty of the state above all others and of positive law to safeguard such rights.

But, more recently, legitimate concern with natural rights has given way to an obsession with the rights of individuals as an end in themselves. 'Human rights' has come to mean the right to have just any need satisfied, however whimsical or capricious. Whereas in the past human rights registered certain fundamental needs and interests – 'fundamental' because indispensable to human flourishing – the clamour for rights extends to practically any need, conceived as such by any individual in any circumstance. Where human rights in the past established a sense of communal identity, they now register subjective perception by endorsing individualistic self-preoccupation. Such a distortion as this, where freedom and toleration are treated as absolutes, however incoherent such a contention may be, as we have seen, is at the root of the increasingly litigious outlook that is so common in the United States. In such an atmosphere, the grounds for grievance expand exponentially, and any who refuse to grant them or, worse, stand in the way of your being granted such 'rights' are your enemies. It matters not that you have translated 'rights' into 'needs' and 'wants' and made yourself the centre of the universe. A sense of social justice was the well-spring from which the reasonable conviction arose that there were such things as human rights. Sadly, in the relatively privileged First World, human rights have now come to mark the claims of individuals to stand aside from social responsibilities and communal identities. But apart from this social context, there is in such a solipsistic world no such thing as a 'right' and certainly no way of adjudicating between conflicting rights. Unrighteous anger is bred all the more easily in such a situation and the conflicts on which it feeds are all the more likely to arise when rights become individually possessed rather than communally shared and communally guarded.

There is one other counterfeit version of righteous anger that masks the deadly sin of wrath in that, under the pretence of justified anger, it seeks to attack and harm some group or individual in a way hardly different from the object of indignation. Not surprisingly, it usually goes hand in hand with hypocrisy: it is righteous indignation. Dorothy L. Sayers pointed to this as the failing of the English particularly. Nowhere is this more evident than in the tawdry newspaper exposés, retailing the peccadilloes and worse of public figures. Under the thin veil of righteous indignation, outpourings of violent language are employed to whip up enmity and hostile reaction. This is the malevolence of the rabble-rouser who seeks out evil not in order to cure it or check it, but to involve others in it, albeit on the side of the persecutor. The quintessential instance of this in recent times must surely be the cynical and cruel way in which National Socialism in Germany made Jews the targets of so-called righteous indignation as the source of the nation's ills, only in order to whip up the wrath of the people into a frenzy of spurious self-protectiveness. The essential sinfulness of the deadly sin of anger is that it aims to do harm, but it does not require that the persons themselves do the harm personally: it merely requires that they stir up the false sense of injustice that provokes violent anger on the part of others.

The only antidote to this deadly sin is offered in the Sermon on the Mount and is perhaps the most strenuous command of the whole of Jesus' moral teaching and the least readily accepted: it is to love your enemies as yourselves. A person may remain your enemy in the sense that he or she intends you harm. But if you strive to love your enemy as you love yourself, whatever harm is done to you, it will not be that harm which turns you into an enemy also. The only alternative to loving your enemy is to retaliate, and while self-defence is permissible and justified, we always run the risk of being corrupted by the resort to violence and thus adopting the role of the aggressor. And where our act of self-defence exceeds what is strictly necessary, we become an unjust aggressor and perpetuate the cycle of violence. To love your enemy as yourself is to recognize one like yourself and to wish no harm. It is to recognize and understand the propensity towards evil with which one is all too familiar within oneself. If we cannot love our enemies it is unlikely that we will be able consistently to love our neighbours as ourselves because exactly the same capacity for empathy is required in both.

THE SEVENTH DEADLY SIN: LUST

And so we finally come to the last of the so-called 'warm-hearted' deadly sins, lust. Lust is usually first in the list of the deadly sins and the one nobody who is asked to rehearse the list forgets. It is unusual to leave it till the last. I started with pride because, of all the deadly sins, pride is the deadliest. Pride engages every aspect and part of us. Moving in every direction, it both reaches into our depths and extends its influence far beyond the confines of our lives. It is the primordial sin, first committed in the Garden of Eden, when two human beings committed the greatest of all follies: they sought to displace their Creator.

But pride is also the most insidious of the deadly sins. It creeps up on us and catches us unawares, it insinuates itself into our judgements and our relationships and masquerades as all manner of virtues, taking whatever form is necessary in order to remain concealed beneath the veneer of respectability and honour and decency that so often afford it house-room.

Lust is at the other end of the spectrum, on all these counts. If pride is the primordial sin, the original sin, that act of madness which cuts us off from our source, then lust is the most conspicuous symptom that things are not as they originally were, both within ourselves and between ourselves. The harmonious ordering of hand, heart and head for which we strive no longer comes naturally to us; instead, we now experience conflict between various aspects of ourselves. Our bodies, and much else besides, feel foreign to us, and intimacy and vulnerability can seem threatening, leading to self-defensiveness. Different appetites and drives seem not to fit easily together and, in the absence of discipline and hard work, they are apt to cause chaos rather than bring happiness.

As with the other 'warm-hearted' sins, lust is the distortion and disordering of a good appetite directed, in other words, towards inappropriate goals. Lust, therefore, puts a vital and valuable aspect of our natures to a use for which it was never intended. The good which it attacks and corrodes is the good which is you and me, human persons, in the fullest sense of those words, built for, and never complete without, love: persons with the capacity for giving and receiving love, unique individuals built for harmonious and generous coexistence with one another. Lust undermines all this, because instead of building up in truthful and trusting intimacy, it involves using other people for our own short-term goals and treating them as means rather than ends in themselves. Lust turns love into a drive to possess and control. It leads us to miss the true goal and settle for a cheap imitation.

The particular aspect of our lives where all this happens is, of course, our sexuality and the reason why lust can be so destructive is that our sexuality is so pervasive and central to our lives. Lust trivializes our sexuality: it is concerned with sex more than sexuality and it proceeds on the fallacious premiss that sex is more important than sexuality. Indeed, lust collapses this distinction altogether, and this is why it constitutes a truncation, a diminution and impoverishment of our natures. Because it treats people, including the person acting lustfully, as objects for use, lust leaves us empty and bereft. Like a drug, it needs another and another and another fix, endlessly searching for but hopelessly missing the point of our sexuality and what it means to be a sexual being.

A healthy sexuality is the single most powerful factor involved in leading a balanced, integrated and flourishing life of selfless happiness. An unhealthy sexuality will most certainly have the opposite effect and impact. Lest there be any confusion here: I do not mean by this statement that you cannot be happy without having sex.

Now whether we realize this or not, our sexuality pervades every aspect of our lives, including the spiritual. It characterizes, distinguishes us from and connects us to all around us in uncountable ways. Our sexuality is an immensely powerful force and drive in our lives and, as such, it is not always easy to manage it in life-giving ways. Its power makes it a formidable force for life and love but, badly managed, it can be an agent of unimaginable unhappiness and destruction. Now, I said that lust fails to distinguish between sexuality and sex. We could put this another way: it fails to distinguish between sexuality and genitality: it acts on the basis that having sex is all there is to sex and it cuts off the groin from the heart.

Sexuality is much, much more than sex or genitality. It is the drive within us for life and all those qualities and conditions that make a full and flourishing life possible: the companionship of friendship, the tenderness of family life and love, the joy, delight and humour of that ease and spontaneous creativity that exists in the trusting, self-forgetfulness of love.

When God said to Adam in Genesis 'It is not good to be alone', he meant it about all of us, whatever our state in life and he meant by it not just physical proximity but that identification and belonging that persists even in solitude. Our sexuality is that energy that works incessantly to re-connect with creation by overcoming the sense of isolation and alienation that has entered into our human existence through the Fall.

Genitality, on the other hand, is only one, albeit very important, aspect of our sexuality. Having sex is a specific fulfilment of this drive in an intimate physical encounter with another human being, most authentic and meaningfully itself when it falls under the rubric of 'making love'.

There are two ways of misunderstanding the significance of genitality. The first way has often seemed to be supported by

Christians in the past and it is often alleged that Catholics in particular still endorse this view. Genital sex must never be downgraded or frowned upon as somehow too messy or earthy to be regarded as part of the spiritual aspect of our natures. This has been the view of many religious sects in history, many of them Christian heresies. For various reasons, these negative views have often been taken to characterize a Christian approach to sex and where these views have been espoused by Christians, it has led not only to hypocrisy and sham but also to missed opportunities for promoting a healthy and enriching theology and spirituality of the body.

Whatever individual Christians have thought and however influential they have been, this negative attitude is the very opposite of a Christian view. Christian teaching does not teach an ideal that consists of a denial of our sexuality in any of its aspects, including the genital. Neurosis, hypocrisy and hardness of heart lie down that road. Christian mystics have freely and famously used the language of erotic love and a whole host of sexual metaphors to describe and hint at the communion with God to which we are called. St Thomas Aquinas unambiguously asserts that sexuality is, in itself, good (*Summa Theologiae* 2a2ae 23.1 *ad* 1) and the lack of due delight in our senses is a serious failing (*ST* 2a2ae 142.1). Indeed, he avers that in man's state of innocence before the fall, the pleasure of sex would have been even greater. (*ST* 1a 98.2 *ad* 3) He is clear that 'People need pleasure as remedies for all sorts of grief and sorrow.' (*ST* 1a2ae 31.5 *ad* 1) and he says that 'To the extent that reasonable activity needs bodily activity he should enjoy bodily pleasures' (*ST* 2a2ae 142.1 *ad* 2). 'Our bodily nature,' he says, 'far from issuing from an evil principle, as the Manichees imagine, is from God' (2a2ae 25.5). According to St Thomas, God has given us our senses so that we might delight in his creation.

The second way in which genitality can be distorted is the opposite of the first. We live in an age that is obsessed not with sexuality but with sex: it is a genitally-fixated age. The view that genitality is the whole of sexuality is popular culture's single most damaging misconception, and it is this that gives rise to the modern myth that you cannot be healthy if you are not having sex – and lots of it.

Now this is inhibiting and, frankly, unimaginative. It has led to the explosion of pornography which has contributed to a jaded and tawdry emptiness, where there should be life, mutual delight and life-giving intimacy. The everything for nothing of the one-night-stand leads to nothing for anybody and to that diminution of our sexual natures so often laid at the door of Christianity. In an oddly paradoxical twist, permissiveness and prudishness arrive at the same impoverishment.

A flourishing and shared life of delight, friendship and love depends on much more than our sleeping arrangements. One can have lots and lots of sex and yet miss out entirely on these indispensable conditions for healthy and wholesome living: living lustily rather than lustfully, we might say. And just as you can have a lot of sex and still lack love and all these other things, so you can be celibate and have all these things in abundance. Having sex does not necessarily ease loneliness. Indeed, empty physical intimacy can make it much worse. You are never more alone than when you are not alone in a loveless and empty show of false intimacy. And there is no lonelier place than a loveless marital bed.

How can we arrive at and maintain a healthy sexuality? Catholics have often been accused of not moving with the times in their teaching on sexuality. Among all Christians in the West, Catholics alone officially hold on to the traditional teaching that contraception is wrong. But in maintaining this position they are consistently holding on to certain traditional Christian principles concerning the whole area of human sexuality and how we are to manage and understand this sacred and God-given aspect of our lives.

Our sexuality is intrinsic to our natures as human beings. Our natures have been created by God and, therefore, our sexuality is a gift of God. This means that sex can never be insignificant, no matter how casually we may treat it on the surface. It will always either build us up or pull us down, enhance life – our life – or diminish it. In a committed, exclusive and permanent relationship it can be life-giving in every sense and a source of growth in trust and love. Conversely, sex that is abstracted from these conditions will bring about the opposite effects. It will harden the heart, trivialize trust, fragment us as human beings and alienate us from one another and ourselves.

Now, popular culture protests that this view accords too much importance to sex: sex, it is said, simply does not carry the significance accorded to it by traditional, Catholic views. The chief factor that has lent plausibility to this popular view of sex is without doubt the advent and widespead use of artificial contraception. Because sex can be sundered from its potential for procreation, many have been led to believe and now act on the conviction that sex no longer touches us at any depth. It is no more psychologically and spiritually significant, in other words, than any other mutually satisfying pastime: hence, widespread talk of 'recreational sex'.

But anybody who holds this view must surely be struck by the strange irony that alongside this view of sexuality must be placed our growing awareness of the socially and personally destructive impact of sex misused. As never before, we are acutely conscious of the tide of suffering caused by sexual abuse of all kinds: incest, rape, infidelity. But it is not just violent, non-consensual sex that damages and destroys: casual, impersonal, uncommitted sex has equally damaging consequences. Sex never happens without some effect and impact, at the time or in due course.

For these reasons, sex is safest (in the fullest possible sense and not just from a modern, hygienic point of view) and therefore most positively significant, in the context of a permanent, all-embracing, exclusive and committed relationship, open to the possibility of new life, in which the free gift of shared intimacy is not inhibited by a desire to avoid the consequences in both biological and psychological terms. And what this amounts to, from a traditional Catholic point of view, is that the genital aspect and expression of our sexuality is best confined to marriage.

By its very nature, sex speaks in its unique bodily language of trust and sharing and mutual commitment through time and in any circumstance: it is the gift of self in the most vulnerable of all human situations. Where these are not present there is inevitably a destructive and damaging dissonance between our deeds and our intentions. Sex in the absence of these conditions is a pretence, a charade, an empty and meaningless gesture, going nowhere and conveying nothing: 'the expense of spirit in a waste of shame'.

Of all aspects of the Catholic Church's teaching on sexuality its position on artificial contraception is, among other Western Christians, distinctive. Its teaching is simply stated: any act of sexual intercourse which involves a conscious and deliberate attempt to frustrate what otherwise might be the potential present in this act for new life renders that act deficient and imperfect, from a moral point of view. It impugns, in other words, the integrity of the act of sexual intercourse between a husband and wife.

Now much has been written and will continue to be written on this topic and I do not intend either to rehearse the well-worn considerations on both sides of the argument or to offer a comprehensive apologia for the Church's teaching. Rather, I want to point to an underlying but rarely remarked assumption that accompanies the view that this teaching is flawed.

The Catholic Church has been accused of callous lack of concern for the many difficulties faced by married couples desperate for good reasons to limit their family size. The Church has also been accused of placing an obstacle in the way of women's liberation from the drudgery and oppression of unwanted childbirth. And she has been reproached with standing in the way of progress in alleviating the plight of the hungry and others in the Third World. Most recently she has been accused of colluding in the spread of AIDS by refusing to endorse the use of condoms between infected people.

Now the clamour against the Church's teaching on contraception as the root of all these ills is premised on the never-articulated but always taken for granted assumption that sex is an indispensable element in everybody's life and, as such, an inalienable right.

Having sex, making love, sometimes leads to new life. If bringing new life into the world is inappropriate or if the circumstances of one's life are unpropitious, then the base line from which every other consideration must begin is that sex is inappropriate where and when bringing new life into the world is also inappropriate. The Catholic Church uniquely holds to the view that intervening in order to disassociate these two momentous aspects of our lives opens up the way to all kinds of developments, both personal and social, that ultimately serve to diminish rather than enhance life. The connection between the widespread use of artificial contraception and the sexualization of society, the breakup of marriage through infidelity, the increase of abortion as a remedy for ineffective contraception, and the inability to offer any rational arguments against the expression of genital sexuality in every and any combination and circumstance, may well as yet be far from easily perceptible and therefore largely unacknowledged, but it is no less real for being unseen.

A final point about a much misunderstood and unfashionable virtue: namely, chastity. 'Chastity' and 'celibacy' are often used interchangeably, but this is to confuse two different things. Celibacy does not mean not having sex, though it entails this. It means not being married. Only because modern society now takes it for granted that sex and marriage are not necessarily or even ideally connected does celibacy come to mean not having sex. In the same way, neither does chastity mean not having sex. A married couple are called to chastity as much as the monk.

Nor does chastity mean being a prude. Being prudish offends against chastity as much as being prurient. In fact, chastity is not primarily concerned with sex. Chastity has to do with the heights and depths of all our experience and all our relationships. It concerns primarily our place in the world and the complex of relationships that locate us in nature and in society and, indeed, it concerns our relationship with ourselves. Chastity concerns primarily reverence and respect for ourselves and others and everything.

To be chaste, therefore, is to relate to others appropriately, freely, respectfully and with integrity, without in any way using or manipulating or invading their own sense of self or their freedom to be themselves. It is to relate, in other words, within appropriate personal, emotional and physical boundaries: that is, within the boundaries set by another person and the truth of their lives. It is to treat other people as ends and never means. We are chaste when we receive and relate to other people in themselves and for themselves, accepting them as they are and for the purposes that give meaning to their lives. Of course, chastity is particularly important in the area of sex because, more easily than any of our other appetites, it can lead us to lose control and offend against another's or our own good by crossing boundaries.

Chastity is misunderstood more than ever. But the alternatives are not conspicuously successful as a remedy for what, it is alleged, chastity and the traditional Catholic teaching on sexuality engender. Which has proved the more effective bulwark against sexual exploitation and abuse and the greater promoter of happiness and stability in families and society at large?

A final point. To fear and dislike sex is as much to be

unchaste as to abuse sex for selfish gratification. Sexual repression is an unambiguous evil which leads to mental imbalance and illness. Chastity protects and enhances the true depth and significance of our sexuality and, as such, it is a virtue that challenges prudery as much as permissiveness. Our aim must be neither to escape nor to exploit our sexuality but to rejoice in and be grateful for our bodily natures so as to be complete and fully alive, living lustily the lives God has given to us.

Lust is a deadly sin in this sense: it leaves us empty-handed and impoverished. This is a truth we all know only too well. In lust, we short-change ourselves, we inflict harm on ourselves and others in place of building up and nourishing what makes for happiness and fullness of life. No one has expressed all this with more insight than Shakespeare.

SONNET CXXIX

The expense of spirit in a waste of shame
Is lust in action; and till action, lust
Is perjur'd, murd'rous, bloody, full of blame,
Savage, extreme, rude, cruel, not to trust;
Enjoy'd no sooner, but despised straight;
Past reason hunted; and no sooner had,
Past reason hated, as a swallow'd bait,
On purpose laid to make the taker mad:
Mad in pursuit, and in possession so;
Had, having, and in quest to have, extreme;
A bliss in proof, and prov'd, a very woe;
Before, a joy propos'd; behind, a dream.
All this the world well knows; and yet none
  Knows well
  To shun the heaven that leads men to this hell.

William Shakespeare

PART IV

The Virtuous Life

INTRODUCING THE VIRTUES

Most of us take it for granted that moral questions typically involve asking whether or not a given course of action is right or wrong. So a typical discussion of some controversial moral issue might concern whether it is right or wrong to use cells from human embryos in experiments or to alleviate disease. Or whether it is right or wrong to infringe the sovereignty of a nation state in order to intervene in some conflict. Or whether it is right or wrong to employ environmentally damaging technologies for short term goals. All these questions concern actions to be done or not to be done.

But freely chosen actions of this kind are done by people; or, better, by persons, human persons. And so it seems reasonable to suggest that there is a more basic kind of moral question to be asked: namely, what is it to be a good person? And, more personally, what kind of person should I become if I want to be a good person? The fact is that such a question as this is always implicit in questions concerning particular actions. So this approach simply makes explicit what is present, whether we aver to it or not, as the background to our questions about which actions are right and which are wrong. And, indeed, without such a background of good and bad, how else can right or wrong make any sense? So rather than beginning with 'What shall I do?', the more fundamental questions to address are, 'What am I?' and 'What ought I to become?' and 'How shall I achieve this goal?'

Now this approach to morality and ethics is known as 'virtue ethics'. And the central point of this approach is that it is concerned primarily not with actions, but with persons and the characteristics which define them as persons. Hence, its most basic enquiry, 'What is a human person?' You cannot know whether something is good or not until you know what it is and what it is supposed to be.

Now there has been a great deal written about this way of understanding. As a general approach, it is significantly different both from the way people have professionally thought about the subject until recently and the way most people on the popular level approach the subject. But this is far from being a new form of ethical enquiry. On the contrary, the current fashion is a return to a much older way of approaching these vital questions, going all the way back to Aristotle in fifth-century Greece and it was the ordinarily accepted way of thinking about these things until roughly the eve of the Protestant Reformation in Europe. It is referred to as 'virtue ethics' because of the original meaning of the word in Greek which our word 'virtue' (from the Latin *virtus*) translates. The Greeks used the word *arete* for anything and everything: an arrow, a vase, an olive grove, a wife, a father, a slave or a citizen. The word means 'excellence' and it was used to register that something was a good example of its kind.

When used of a person, *arete* refers to the characteristics of the good person: good in the sense of being all that a person is meant to be. Hence the necessity of asking what precisely a person is meant to be. Now when Aristotle asks himself what a good person is, he is necessarily confined within a highly specific and historically conditioned set of categories and expectations. For one thing, he is asking about what it is to be a good *man*. And this is because his conception of human flourishing concerned the citizens of the Greek city-state, the *polis*. And only men, not women, and free men, not slaves, were citizens. So when Aristotle answers this question he offers eleven different virtues vital to the life of the good citizen. For Aristotle, a human being is first and foremost a social being, taking his part in the life of the *polis*. And he is a rational being, able to exercise his faculty for right thinking and clear argument. Of course, he has much more to say besides. But for our purpose we can see the methodology involved. First ask what kind of thing a person is and what they are for – what is their *telos*, or their purpose. And then you are in a position to say what characteristics a good specimen of this kind of thing will display – what, in other words, constitutes the virtuous person, the person who is all that he or she is meant to be.

Now I said that there is a widespread revival of interest in this way of thinking about ethics. But, at their best, Catholic ways of doing ethics and moral theology have always been along these lines. And it is commonly acknowledged, and not just by Catholics, that the foremost exponent of this approach to ethics and morality since the thirteenth century has been St Thomas Aquinas. Catholic and other ways of doing ethics have fallen on hard times usually when they have failed to make capital from these insights.

When we talk about the virtues, then, we are answering the question 'What kind of person should I become?' They are the goal towards which we strive, even if we never become fully that kind of person perfectly in this life. A distinct advantage of this approach to ethics, therefore, is that one of its fundamental categories is growth. Ethics is concerned, on this reading, with knowing what we should aim to become and setting ourselves in the *direction* of the goal. But arriving there is a long process. Indeed, Aristotle makes the point succinctly and memorably that this is a lifetime's work when he says, 'One swallow does not make a summer, nor one fine day.'

Another advantage of this approach over the action-oriented understanding of ethics is that it attends to the whole person and to the whole of a person's life. Remembering that growth is the key concept, this approach acknowledges that every moment and every circumstance can contribute to the growth of virtue or its opposite. And this is based on the view that every free act has its effect and contributes to the kind of person you and I become. I become, in other words, what I do. Or as Gerard Manley Hopkins has it, 'What I do is me.'

One way of describing the difference between these two ways of doing ethics is to say that one is problem-based and the other person-based. The problem-based approach responds and reacts to situations as and when they arise, while the other approach is pro-active and cultivates the inner person from which the outer actions emanate.

Now when Aquinas asks himself what virtues characterize a good human being, he comes up with seven. And this is because, needless to say, while he agrees with almost all of what Aristotle thinks constitutes a good human being, he has a considerably enlarged view of what human persons are. Included in Aristotle's list of virtues are what are known even now as the cardinal virtues – coming from the Latin *cardo*, a hinge – which are Prudence, Justice, Fortitude, and Temperance. These four virtues constituted the cornerstones of civic rectitude for Greeks and

Romans. They are found also in the Hebrew tradition (see the Book of Wisdom) and, as such, they are the foundation of the moral consciousness of the ancient world. But of course how these are to be interpreted changes subtly with the setting in which they are being discussed. Clearly, in Aristotle's case, as we have seen, they are explained in the context of civic existence in the city-state.

Aristotle includes these in his list of eleven virtues and Aquinas also includes them, as did St Augustine before him, in his description of the good man. But whereas for Aristotle the overarching goal and purpose of man is to take his place as a rational being in the life of the city, for Aquinas man is made in the image and likeness of God: he is built, not only for reason but for love, and he thus has a goal and purpose which far exceed the expectations of Aristotle and his contemporaries. That goal is nothing less than communion with God: in other words, friendship with God, which naturally includes friendship and communion among men.

So Aquinas interprets the four cardinal virtues in terms of this goal. And in doing this he adds three other virtues to the other four which serve to root them in the love of God. To the cardinal virtues of Prudence, Justice, Fortitude and Temperance, Aquinas adds the so-called 'theological' virtues of Faith, Hope and Charity. But these three differ in marked ways from the others: they are not acquired in the same way as the other virtues and they have an entirely different object. The cardinal virtues are acquired by repeated, freely chosen and enjoyed habitual actions. The theological virtues, on the other hand, are infused; that is to say, they are gifts of God's grace, not the result of human effort. Secondly, the cardinal virtues have as their object the human person: they make us into a particular kind of person. The theological virtues, on the other hand, have as their object God himself and by effecting union between us and God, the communion of love, they make us friends of God. And it's to the first of these, faith, that we turn.

FAITH

'To acquire knowledge about God is one thing; to commit oneself to him is another.'[33] Latin has two words for faith: *fides* and *fiducia*. *Fides* concerns 'belief that . . . ' and *fiducia* 'belief in . . . ' Alternative translations of the second, less familiar of these words would be 'trust' or 'commitment'. *Fides* has for its object one or more propositions. *Fiducia* has for its object a person. In the Catholic view of things, both of these aspects are necessarily part of the meaning of the theological virtue of faith.

Of these two elements, however, faith in the sense of *fiducia* has been more frequently discussed recently. And this, of course, is consistent with the more modern tendency to emphasize the place and role of feelings and the affective element in persons. Ever since the Romantic Movement and further supported by Existentialism in the inter-war period, inner conviction as the well-spring of action and authenticity as the goal of action have been powerful shapers of the way we understand ourselves.

Another, rather more negative, reason for the emphasis on faith as trust is the embarrassment felt by some Christians ever since the Enlightenment that faith, unlike science, was and is lacking in 'cognitive stability'.[34] Faith, in other words, became the poor relation, compared with the bold new strides made by the sciences. This has led many over the years to resort to strictly non-cognitive accounts of religious faith in the hope, largely illusory, of rescuing faith from its allegedly embarrassing inferiority to science.

But, though the relationship between *fides* and *fiducia* is complex and dynamic, the notion of *fiducia* without *fides* is vacuous and dangerous. Sheer *fiducia* can have anything or nothing as its object and is therefore always open to the danger of fanaticism in the absence of any regulative, cognitive element.

Faith is customarily distinguished from knowledge. But this has often led to an unwarranted dichotomy. Now we can accept the distinction without necessarily accepting the dichotomy. In so far as there is a distinction, therefore, between faith and knowledge, we might say, provisionally, that it corresponds, at least in part, to the difference between cognition and recognition.

Knowledge understood as certainty patient of proof is comparatively rare outside of the analytic truths of mathematics and logic. There is good reason to believe that not even scientific knowledge, as such, ever arrives at complete certainty. Indeed, the notion of complete factual certainty, like the idea of complete scepticism, is unintelligible and impracticable, if taken in an unqualified sense. As Alasdair MacIntyre once said, facts, like telescopes and wigs for gentlemen, were an invention of the seventeenth century.

Further, in our everyday lives, certainty of this kind plays a comparatively unimportant role. We work with provisional knowledge in most situations. Those things about which we claim certainty always go beyond the empirical. This kind of certainty is better represented as conviction; as such it is something in which we grow over time.

In practice, nobody can limit themselves to factual, empirically testable knowledge of the kind vaunted by the Logical Positivists. Most of everyday life is built around beliefs of a trivial kind and convictions of a critical kind. The former concern what has been called 'the world about us' and the latter concern 'the world'.[35] The chief difference between these two kinds of belief consists in their different relationship to the idea of evidence.

Our beliefs concerning 'the world about us' are derived from the appraisal of empirical evidence by ourselves or authoritative others. Such beliefs stand or fall on empirical evidence of one kind or another, immediate or remote. But though empirical and other kinds of evidence are relevant to our convictions or beliefs concerning 'the world', in a strictly corroborative or confirmatory way, such convictions do not normally stand or fall according to this kind of evidence.

This is related to the fact that, though we ourselves are part of 'the world about us' and therefore can know about this or that feature of it, we are at the same time possessed of a drive: 'an impulse and capacity to transcend [our] particular point of view and to conceive of the world as a whole'.[36] But we find ourselves in a tension between both the inside and the outside point of view which constitute these two perspectives. We can no more step out of our world than we can step out of our heads to gain an overall vantage point from which to get a clear, objective view. Our views of 'the world' will necessarily be arrived at differently from any view we may entertain of 'the world about us', since the former forms the context within which or the horizon against which we locate and situate all our views of 'the world about us'. Such foundational beliefs as these will not be arrived at by relentless logic or empirical scrutiny or intellectual effort alone.

What is more, however much we may seek to confine ourselves to testable knowledge, ultimate questions persist and are answered more by our lives (values, priorities, moral decisions, etc.) than by our words. We cannot live without adopting a view of the whole, whether implicitly or explicitly. It is therefore a tendentious caricature to imagine the world divided into believers and unbelievers. It is a world divided among those who hold different beliefs.

The alternative view has perhaps arisen for the same reasons as the reduction of faith to commitment: namely, a Post-Enlightenment nervousness about the cognitive credentials of belief, and of religious faith in particular. Within such a perspective, believers have conceded the rationalist contention that belief is an inferior kind of knowledge: something provisional until it can be 'firmed-up' into knowledge. But this concession merely confirms the 'scientistic' distortion that sees science as the sole and exclusive paradigm of true knowledge. Many now question this as a just estimate of scientific knowledge in its own right. But there is ample reason to question this scenario quite apart from considerations internal to science itself.

Most crucially, this false scenario offers a quite unrealistic view of the role of belief in all our knowledge. Belief is not just a vague, hopeful approximation to true knowledge. It is crucial to all knowledge and, indeed, all human life. It is even crucial to the enterprise of science itself and certainly to the notion of scientific progress. The scientist starts off from an indispensable belief in the order and intelligibility of the universe: he does not arrive at this conviction as a result of his researches.

All intellectual activity, whether empirical or logical, entails starting-points and first principles which are not themselves the fruit of such activity but its very presupposition. Even in the day-to-day exercise of reason and the search for knowledge, the drive to further knowledge and understanding presupposes beliefs of various kinds. Without such dispositions, which are more aptly described as beliefs, thought and reasoning would never strive to transcend any given position already arrived at. Belief opens us to the future, stretches us beyond ourselves, and secures goals and ideals. It is for this reason that Leszek Kolakowski describes the Augustinian-Anselmian formula *credo ut intelligam* – 'I believe in order that I may understand' as a methodological principle 'that operates over the whole field of knowledge'.[37] When we turn to the field of human relationships and social existence, the role of belief is even more obviously critical to the very existence of human beings in everything they do and strive to become.

Nevertheless, though evidence is never sufficient to establish it, belief is never in total separation from the corroboration and confirmation of evidence. Belief is not blind or impetuous. It is associated with reflection and reasoning and it must be both responsible and reasonable. There are on offer many reduction-ist accounts of faith and religious belief. None of us can deny the role of factors outside ourselves (of a sociological kind) and within ourselves (of a psychological kind) in influencing our beliefs. Accidents of birth and circumstance as well as emotion-al and temperamental predispositions all play their part in the make-up and origin of our beliefs. But none of these factors is, strictly speaking, relevant to the truth or falsity of our beliefs. There is a nervousness on the part of believers who feel them-selves uniquely bound to offer explanations of their beliefs and therefore uniquely vulnerable to explanations of belief that dwell on the genesis of belief: where, in other words, the belief comes from. No such so-called 'genetic' account of the origin of any particular belief can finally settle the question of its truth or falsity.

There is undoubtedly as much possibility of wishful thinking or projection on the part of those who hold beliefs other than religious ones, whether opposed or not, as there is on the part of religious believers. A commitment to rationality is required by all parties if arbitrariness and subjectivism is to be avoided.[38] But this is simply to say that we must in all things, including reli-gious belief and faith, exercise our critical faculties. And this is very different from espousing the principles of narrow rational-ism.

We can now turn to religious faith specifically. All know-ledge, as we saw, is corporate and communal. None of us can detach any knowledge or belief we possess from the context of tradition, society and community, presently and historically. All our understanding is gained in dialogue with tradition.[39] We must ask ourselves: what is the essential, fundamental object of belief in the sense of both *fides* and *fiducia*? In a Christian context the answer must be: God, who is the providential creator and sustainer of my life and all existence.

Now I can ask two quite different kinds of questions of this belief: first, how did I come to believe it to be true? And, secondly, why do I believe it to be true? It may be that in asking these questions I realize that they have the same answer and this may result in my coming to the conviction that I do not personally hold this belief to be true. But it may well be that while a partial answer to the first can be offered (say, in terms of birth and circumstances) it cannot be answered fully to our satisfaction. As regards the second question, it may be that we find ourselves in a quandary. Our answers seem fragmentary and unsatisfactory. I find myself able to offer many partial but no complete justifications.

Am I to take this as a counter-indication and thus suspend belief until I arrive at some illusory certainty? It seems to me not so. Consider the similarities between this second question about why you believe in God and the following questions: why do you believe in the order and intelligibility of the universe and therefore the desirability of living reasonably? Why do you believe in a moral existence as an ideal, as opposed to living at random? Why do you believe in love, its existence and the possibility and desirability of living accordingly?

The late Bernard Lonergan has some illuminating remarks on the nature of religious faith.[40] In religious faith man sees not himself as the origin of value and the goal of love and goodness, but God. But such a conviction is necessarily a 'knowledge' which goes beyond experiencing, understanding and judging: it is an intentional response to a transcendent value. That is, a value which places all other values and all other knowledge in its own perspective. It is an ordering horizon. It is the kind of knowledge 'reached through discernment of value and the judgements of value of a person in love'. In this sense, 'Faith is the knowledge born of religious love'. And we may add with St Paul: 'the love of Christ which surpasses all knowledge'.[41]

God reveals himself in history. Historical reality is the vehicle, and historical awareness will necessarily enter into the meaning of what is revealed and cannot be ignored if there is to be an appropriate understanding of what is revealed. And yet what is revealed cannot be measured by the historical reality.[42]

There is a parallel here with the role of language in matters of faith. The revelation is necessarily expressed in language, yet it would be a great mistake – and one not always successfully avoided – to imagine that the revelation is co-terminous with the language. Language is a vehicle. And yet, at the same time, the revelation is inconceivable without language.

Rational criticism and exploration are a necessity not a luxury in matters of faith and what is proposed for faith must be reasonable. Reason is therefore not a prolegomenon to faith but its permanent accompaniment. Nevertheless, in order to appreciate the relationship between reason and faith, it is as important to avoid an understanding of reason which confines it within the canons of mathematical integrity as it is to avoid an understanding of faith which confines it to blind and unreasonable assertion independent of argument. We must set ourselves to find reason in mystery and mystery in reason. Logic and mystery belong together, and faith is the name for that gift of the spirit which understands God as the origin of both.

HOPE

There is a venerable theological principle which states: *lex orandi, lex credendi.* This is a way of saying that the Church's faith is expressed primarily in her liturgy. In other words, if you want to know what Christians believe find out how and for what they pray.

Now one of the most ancient prayers in the Roman liturgy is the one that is said by the priest after the Our Father. 'Deliver us, Lord, from every evil, and grant us peace in our day. In your mercy keep us free from sin and protect us from all anxiety as we wait in joyful hope for the coming of our Saviour, Jesus Christ.' For our present purpose, the three important elements mentioned are: peace, freedom from sin and anxiety, and joyful hope. And what roots this prayer is the 'coming of our Saviour'.

Anxiety is no respecter of persons and, whatever else divides human beings one from another, we are united in finding within ourselves a deep-seated restlessness and an unfulfilled yearning which enters into every corner and crevice of human life. And yet we are indomitable in our search for whatever it is that will meet this need and quiet this restlessness. Dr Johnson used the phrase 'the triumph of hope over experience' to describe second marriages. But his witticism nicely catches the situation we all find ourselves in. Even in the face of hard experience we persist in our search for a love that lasts and a security and happiness that is endless and complete, safe from the passage of time or the vicissitudes of fortune.

Yet, though we all share this restlessness and yearning, we are by no means all agreed about its meaning. Many of us all of the time and all of us some of the time mistake it for some finite desire or need. And so we set out to find and possess that which we imagine our heart desires. We fondly imagine, in other words, that there is something we can do or achieve or possess that will satisfy and fulfil this desire. Consequently, it is the repeated experience of many that whatever we do to satisfy this longing it remains always a partial and temporary solution, no matter how intense and enjoyable the particular experience in question may be. However much we bury ourselves in our work or business; however much we seek comfort in worldly success or indulgence, always the peace we achieve remains vulnerable to fortune or circumstance and never, in practice, lasts. Even the greatest fortune of all, the love of one person for another, carries with it the pain of eventual loss. So, in every human experience, whether painful or happy, there is always an intimation of lack.

A key element in our lived faith is our awareness of the contrast between human expectation and possibility, on the one hand, and the mystery of God's ways, on the other. And what holds this contrast before our eyes, enabling us to place our trust in the life God has given us and live life to the full, at ease in his creation, is the theological virtue of hope.

Notice, the virtue of hope has nothing to do with shallow and randomly superficial optimism: such an attitude as this can be merely the accidental result of temperament or the desired result of a refusal to face reality. On the contrary, hope is rooted in God alone and it gives rise to a confidence that the whole of our lives and the whole of creation is encompassed by and taken up into an inconceivable and infinite Love. The virtue of hope, a gift of God's grace not the product of the human will, keeps before us the possibility, by grace, that this yearning will be fulfilled, completely, by God.

Nor is hope a subtle form of escapism or a sidewards glance of anticipation. It goes hand in hand with hard realism about ourselves and our inadequacies and it persists in the emptiness of disappointment and suffering, and even sin. No number of frustrated hopes or unfulfilled dreams can cancel Christian hope. Nor is hope concerned solely with the future, as if we were resigned to a hard time now as long as things are going to get better. It is the hallmark of a new life now. This new life in Christ, with all its daily dying to self as well as our eventual physical death, is even now to be lived generously and joyously, because it is lived in hope.

But far from being just a natural virtue or the happy outcome of an optimistic temperament or disposition, hope is a gift of God. Its grounds and foundation would otherwise be hidden from us if God did not open our eyes to the truth in which it is rooted; and no amount of ingenuity or effort or training can generate that trust and confidence which is Christian hope. All Christian hope rests in one who is not defeated by what defeats us. It looks to the God of grace who gives himself to us, dealing both with our guilt and then with all that weakens our creaturely power to be. Christ himself and his proven love for us is the sole adequate grounds of hope. And the sacraments of Christian life reassure us that he stands in our midst, before us and beside us, at all times and for ever.

And what do we hope for? Our hope is rooted in the knowledge that God will take us through death and final judgement and then renew us in power for a life of glory, where all experience will be a participation in God's own joy. To believe in God is to hope, and hope sets us free to love, and love overcomes everything.

LOVE – AND DO WHAT YOU WILL

The title of this final chapter is a direct quotation from one of the greatest figures of Christian history and the most influential thinker in Western Christianity, St Augustine of Hippo (354-430). Augustine's life covered some of the most dramatic and decisive events in the history of the world so far. During his lifetime the ever-quickening decline of the Roman Empire in the

West came to a head as province after province collapsed and fell into the hands of barbarian invaders. It is almost impossible for us now to conceive the psychological impact this had on the minds of Augustine and his contemporaries, pagans and Christians alike. It was no less than the threatened collapse of the known world. It has been suggested that the nearest equivalent would be to hear news that a nuclear war had begun, with the realization that civilization as we know it was on the brink of collapse.

In his own personal life also Augustine experienced all the vicissitudes of human existence: he searched for the answers to perplexing problems and thought he had found them, only to suffer the disappointment of realizing their inadequacy. He struggled with his own temperament and particularly with his very strong sexual appetites – it was he who prayed for chastity in the famous words: *Da mihi, Domine, castitatem: sed non iam.* 'Lord, give me chastity, but not yet.' He lived with a woman he loved and had an equally beloved son by her, but then suffered the trauma of separating from her after seventeen years of marriage in everything but name. I mention all this in order to stress the immense authority these words have, coming as they do from such a distinguished and influential saint. But, though these words have immense power, Augustine was simply being faithful to the Christian tradition when he said them.

In our own time, love has become a difficult word to use well. It is, without doubt, the most common word in the popular songs of every generation and every country. Love, we are told, is all you need: it is the solution to all our problems. And with this, as we have seen, our Lord, St Paul and the great St Augustine would agree. But since the word is used now in ways that differ radically from each other, we need to be clear about what this magical word means.

There can be no more overworked noun or verb. The word means both too much and too little. It can be and has been used to mean almost anything. And, indeed, it has been used to justify much that is plainly abhorrent. At times the appeal to love can be both trivial and lethal. And yet it is precisely this word, with all its potential ambiguity, that is offered by the Lord himself as the summation of the law and the prophets. The entire purpose and will of God for our lives is expressed by this word 'love'.

> **'Teacher, which commandment in the law is the greatest?' He said to him, 'You shall love the Lord your God with all your heart, and with all your soul, and with all your mind.' This is the greatest and first commandment. And the second is like it: 'You shall love your neighbour as yourself.' On these two commandments hang all the law and the prophets.**
>
> (Matt. 22:36–40)

Now, the answer our Lord gives to those who try to trick him is not as earth-shatteringly original as it might seem. He is quoting directly from the great Shema, the prayer recited by devout Jews every morning and night: the command to love God absolutely was to be 'written on the heart' and drilled into the memory of every child. The second part of the response – 'You shall love your neighbour as yourself' – is from the Book of Leviticus. Again, not original.

But what *is* original and what would have raised eyebrows is the fact that Jesus puts both of these commands on an equal footing. You *can't* love God and, at the same time, harbour in your heart hatred of even one person. To love God *is* to love your neighbour: there is no other way. And this extraordinary identification of love of neighbour with love of God runs throughout the Gospels.

Clearly, then, the word 'love' is not entirely without content, not infinitely plastic: it involves some things and excludes others. It involves heart and will, soul and life, mind and strength. It requires fidelity and makes demands. It is as arduous as it is ardent.

Of course, we sometimes mistake other things for love. We often find ourselves anxious for the love and regard of others, feeding on it, demanding it, ensuring people's attention is focused on us. We encourage others to rely on us, to depend on us, never to be free of us, and think we are loving them, whilst all the time we are using them as props for our own weakness and fear of rejection.

But genuine love surrenders even the desire to be loved in return. It allows the one who is loved to become themselves. And for this, love must be able to let be and to let go. It is the very opposite of self-centredness, actively seeking the good of the one loved before one's own and yet, paradoxically, finding one's own good in the process. When love is mutual the good of each becomes the good of the other, neither dominating nor cultivating dependence, never standing still but permanently open to the possibility of growth.

Am I being idealistic? No. One often hears St Paul's passage about love read at weddings: Love is patience, kindness, it is not jealous or conceited, rude or selfish. It does not take offence, nor is it resentful. It is always ready to trust, to excuse, to forgive and to endure whatever comes. I often think this should be reserved for the crisis times of marriage, not the beginning, to bring people back to a sense of realism.

Being in love is easy, given the right circumstances. But love is different. It is unconditional: it depends on nothing, save the other person's existence. When we experience that kind of love, however seemingly inauspicious the circumstances, however different from the expectations of others, we are in the presence of God, enfolded by his love.

St Augustine could say, 'Love and do what you will' because genuine love fulfils every law: it is the perfection of the image and likeness of God in which we are made. Nothing can be lacking where there is love. And only love leads to God because genuine love is from God. It is not a human adornment we can acquire or appropriate. It is sheer gift, from God and ultimately for God. As all genuine love is from God, so God is the completion of all love. Those whom we love, we love in God, not alongside him.

We become what we love and only love unites us to God. Love therefore is at the heart of the Christian life and no outward achievement or any other gift counts for anything if there is no love.

Let me end with the full quotation from St Augustine:

> **Love, and do what you will. If you keep silence, keep silence in love; if you speak, speak in love; if you correct, correct in love; if you forbear, forbear in love. Let love's root be within you, for from that root nothing but good can spring.**
>
> *(Ep. Joannis 7.8)*

Conclusion

When he called the Second Vatican Council, Pope John XXIII famously used the word *aggiornamento* to describe the point and purpose of his momentous initiative. Bringing the Church 'up to date' best translates the word he used. To many who disagreed, then and now, with the Council's work, this seemed a singularly inappropriate goal: how could the unchanging Church, with its unchanging message of salvation, need bringing up to date?

At the opposite extreme, there were those, then and now, who saw the Council as an opportunity to strip away all that was inessential, and effect a return to the pristine state of innocence and clarity which they fondly imagined characterized the golden age of the early Church.

As so often happens with seemingly opposed views at the extreme, both these positions have much in common. Both are unacceptable and unhelpful; and both are premised on a misunderstanding of the nature of the Church. Each of these views fails to realize that the Church's faith is both unchanging and ever-changing. The object of its faith is God, incarnate in Jesus Christ. Christianity is not a religion of the book but of the person, a particular person: Jesus Christ, God and man. And the goal of our lives is unchanging: namely, communion with God, sharing his life.

But we human beings are historical, rooted in time and language. And therefore the Church's articulation of its faith evolves as human languages evolve and human experience expands. From the very beginning Christians sought to render their faith intelligible in the thought-forms and language of their own culture not only to those outside the Church but to themselves. The engagement of the mind in appropriating and understanding the faith gave rise to theology: an activity of the intellect in which, according to St Anselm and St Augustine before him, faith seeks understanding.

The faith is not a fossilized relic from a long past era: it is a living reality, concretely realized in the context of real life in the real world, confronting and illuminating the human situation at its limits. The tendency to canonize and set in stone any period of the Church's life in its external forms or any particular historically conditioned expression of its teaching is harmful. Implacable resistance to change is as damaging as irresponsible change for change's sake. Cardinal Newman's much-quoted words are appropriate here:

> **Whatever the risk of corruption from intercourse with the world around, such a risk must be encountered if a great idea is fully to be understood and much more if it is to be fully exhibited . . . It is indeed sometimes said that the stream is clearer near the spring. Whatever may be fairly made of this image, it does not apply to the history of a philosophy or a belief, which on the contrary is more equable, and purer, and stronger, when its bed has become deep, and broad, and full . . . In time it enters upon strange territory; points of controversy alter their bearing; parties rise and fall around it; dangers and hopes appear in new relation; and old principles reappear under new forms. It changes with them in order to remain the same. In a higher world it is otherwise, but here below to live is to change, and to be perfect is to have changed often.[43]**

Many characterizations of Catholicism in the recent past dwelt on the unchanging nature of the Church as its most attractive quality. For many, the changes of the Vatican Council were a disappointment, unpicking what appeared to them as a seamless tapestry, ever the same and ever one in thought and custom. This was not objection to any particular change, but to change itself. But this failed to take into account the verifiable historical fact that the Church's external forms and her understanding of herself have evolved over its history and on many occasions in the past have changed radically.

The first of these shifts came when the early Church moved away from its Jewish beginnings and encountered the Hellenistic world at large. The early parts of the New Testament, especially the Acts of the Apostles and Paul's letters, reflect the efforts and the turmoil involved in accommodating and expanding the convictions of the early Church to a new cultural environment. In general, what we see there is the attempt to distinguish what is essential and central from what is secondary and peripheral. This effort to open the door of faith to all continued with the second-century Apologists who sought to defend Christian faith before those who regarded it as alien and unreasonable. Again, figures such as Justin Martyr sought to show that Christianity was consistent with all that was good in the world and society and they consciously looked for ways of translating the claims of Christianity in order to render them intelligible to their contemporaries. The climax of this movement is reached with the magisterial figure of St Augustine of Hippo who strove to show, among much else, that Christian faith is consistent with whatever is good in pagan culture and that its claims are not compromised even in the face of the cataclysmic collapse of the Roman world in the West.

Again, in the twelfth and thirteenth centuries huge changes in the articulation of faith took place as newly recovered philosophical texts of Aristotle offered an opportunity to present faith in terms of a new intellectual framework and scientific outlook. None of this happened without controversy and struggle and even figures now universally recognized as bulwarks of orthodoxy, such as St Thomas Aquinas, were regarded with suspicion in their own day as a result of their efforts to meet the challenge of the intellectual revolution happening around them. But it was precisely because Aquinas was so thoroughly immersed in the tradition that he was able to engage in such brilliant innovation.

We in the twenty-first century find ourselves in the midst of the another period of change and development on all fronts, another transformation of Western culture. So-called postmodernity, characterized by pluralism and relativism, where truth is no longer a fixed goal but plural and changing, a fluid, language-generated facet of a particular culture and time, is seen by some as incompatible with Christian orthodoxy, while still others see it as an opportunity for reopening theological questions and sensibilities that have been dormant since the Enlightenment.

Exactly the same division of opinion was to be found in each of the periods of change already referred to in the early Church and the Middle Ages: there were vociferous Christian voices raised in both situations to warn against any association with or research into contemporary intellectual developments. In the past, those who took the trouble to immerse themselves in both the tradition of faith, with the theology to which it gave rise, and the fruits of intellectual and all other human labours, proved themselves in a better position to engage in the perennial task facing Chrisianity: namely, to render intelligible the hope and faith received for the benefit of all, without exception. This will always be, of course, much more than a solely intellectual exercise, but it can never happen without the mind's engagement with the questions and achievements of humankind. Exactly the same exigence was expressed by the author of the First Letter of Peter: 'Be always ready to speak for the hope that is in you to any who call upon you, but do it with gentleness and reverence' (1 Peter 3:15).

Notes

1. 'Beware', he says in the letter to the Colossians, 'lest anybody spoll you through philosophy and vain deceit.' (Colossians 2:8). And his ambiguous attitude is seen at the Areopagus where he freely quotes Greek poets and tries to speak of Christian faith in terms intelligible to his sophisticated Greek audience. Acts 17:28. The saying, 'In him we live and move and have our being' may be modelled on one of Epimenides of Knossos (6th cent. BC) and the poet he quotes from is the 3rd century Cilician, Aratus of Soli or Tarsus.

2. *De praescriptione haereticorum*, vii, 2-3 (ed. Refoule, *Corpus Christianorum*, Series Latina Vol. 1, 92,4-7). Cited by Norman Kretzmann, 'Reason in Mystery' in G. Vesey (ed.) *The Philosophy in Christianity*, Cambridge, 1989, pp.15-40, p.20.

3. See John Dillon, 'Logos and Trinity: Patterns of Platonist Influence on Early Christianity', in Vesey, *op. cit.*, 1–14, p.1.

4. See Michael Haren, *Medieval Thought: the Western Intellectual Tradition from Antiquity to the 13th Century*, London, 1985, p. 1.

5. Fergus Kerr, 'The Need for Philosophy in Theology Today' in *New Blackfriars* 65 (1984) 768, p. 249.

6. Based on Austin Farrer, 'The Christian Apologist' in Gibb, *Light on C. S. Lewis*, London, 1965, p. 26.

7. Bernard Lonergan, *Philosophy of God and Theology*, London, 1973, p. 50.

8. Nicholas Lash, 'Observation, Revelation, and the Posterity of Noah' in Russell, Stoeger and Coyne (eds), *Physics, Philosophy and Theology*, Vatican City and Notre Dame, 1988, pp. 210ff.

9. Donald Mackinnon, 'The Inexpressibility of God' in *Theology* LXXIX (1976) 670, p. 201.

10. *ST* 2a2ae 1.3.

11. *Themes in Theology*, Edinburgh, 1966, pp. 143–4.

12. Hans Urs von Balthasar, 'The Unknown God' in *Elucidations*, p. 23.

13. Nicholas Lash, *op. cit.*, pp. 203–219, p. 211.

14. David Hume, Dialogues concerning Natural Religion, in *Hume on Religion*, ed. Richard Wolheim, London, 1971, p. 172.

15. Herbert McCabe, *God Matters*, London, 1987, p. 29.

16. McCabe, *op. cit.*, p. 35.

17. *De Veritate* 16.2; 17.2.

18. Don Cupitt, *Creation out of Nothing*, London, 1990, pp. 15–16.

19. Cupitt, *op. cit.*, p. 60.

20. Aidan Nichols, *Epiphany: a Theological Introduction to Catholicism*, Minnesota, 1996, p. 466.
21. Nichols, *op. cit.*, p. 467.
22. McCabe, *op. cit.*, p. 7.
23. Nicholas Lash, 'On Watching Our Language About God' in *Priests and People*, 7 (1993) 10, 371--5, p. 375.
24. Nicholas Lash in Russell, Coyne and Stoeger, p. 209.
25. Cupitt, *op.cit.* p. 60.
26. Dorothy L. Sayers, *Creed or Chaos*, New York 1949.
27. Sayers, *op. cit.*, p. 108.
28. Mary Midgley, *Wisdom, Information and Wonder*, London, 1989, p. 35.
29. Midgley, *op. cit.*, pp. 34–5.
30. *De catechizandis rudibus*, 4,8: PL 40, 315–16.
31. *Moralia* in Job, 31,45: PL 76, 621.
32. *Murder in the Cathedral*, Part I, p. 238 in *Collected Works*.
33. Romanus Cessario, *Christian Faith and the Theological Life*, Washington, 1996, p. 1.
34. This phrase is taken from Janet Soskice, 'Knowledge and Experience in Science and Religion: Can We Be Realists?' in Russell, Stoeger and Coyne (eds), *op. cit.*, p. 176.
35. See Chris Cherry in an unpublished paper, 'The World and the World about us'.
36. Thomas Nagel, *The View from Nowhere*, Oxford, 1986, p. 3.
37. Leszek Kolakowski, *Religion*, London 1982, p. 84.
38. Based on a remark by Michael Polanyi, cited by Ian Barbour in 'Ways of Relating Science and Religion' in Russell, Stoeger and Coyne (eds), *op. cit.*, p. 39.
39. This is MacIntyre's point. See also Soskice, *op.cit.*, p. 179. See also Andrew Louth, *Discerning the Mystery*, Oxford, 1983, p. 33: 'Understanding is an engagement with tradition, not an escape from it.'
40. Bernard Lonergan, *Method in Theology*,London,1972, pp.115–18.
41. Eph. 3:19.
42. This point is based on Austin Farrer in 'Faith and Reason' in *Reflective Faith*, London, 1972.
43. *An Essay on the Development of Christian Doctrine*, London, 1906, p. 40.

Index